Split in Two

Reconciled through Yoga

Applause for Split in Two

Ann's captivating story begins in the early 1950's with her parents who are active in the American Communist party. As the FBI closes in, they are required to escape with their children in the middle of the night behind the Iron Curtain in Prague, Czechoslovakia. When disillusioned with the Czech version of communism her parents follow their dream by moving the family to Mao's China. The uprooted children leave behind an established identity, a language, contact with extended family and friends. When back in the US adult Ann begins the work of integrating her experiences of uprootedness and loss. Urged by a friend to take a yoga class Ann begins an ever-deepening journey that challenges her to open to the past through a re-connection to her body. Following her heart and deepening her practice leads her to the Kripalu Center for Yoga and Health. Her descriptions of Kripalu and the Teacher Training program will resonate with everyone who has shared those experiences. Ann's story reveals the power of a yoga practice to heal the wounds of the body and mind.

Yoganand, Michael Carroll
senior faculty at the Kripalu Yoga Center

Split in Two, by Ann Kimmage, moves between memory and moment as the author discovers yoga at the age of 57 and begins a journey of integration. Kimmage intertwines present moment experiences on her mat with difficult memories from a childhood raised in exile as the daughter of Communist parents who fled behind the Iron Curtain during the height of the Red Scare in the 1950s. A humble yogini who believed she was too old to first do yoga and then teach it, what Kimmage - and the reader - discover in this rich and vulnerable narrative is a pathway to wholeness that begins with the breath, followed by the body, and down the long road to remembering the places that hurt with compassion and care. "Split in Two" is a memoir for anyone interested in personal integration, and especially for those who might feel it's too late. Kimmage assures us that it never is.

Raye S. Leonard
Editor, *The Lincoln County News*

For all of us striving to nourish ourselves and find balance in life, Ann Kimmage's latest book is an inspiration. Genuinely and without ego, she delivers the fascinating story of her traumatic family life--the struggles for belonging amid the repeated disruptions in her childhood that continued to impact her in adult life. The astute descriptions, keenly perceived details, and resonant dialogue will keep readers wanting to turn the page.

Donna Marshall
Executive Director of Midcoast Senior College

Split in Two

Reconciled through Yoga

a memoir

Ann Kimmage

PUBLISHING

Ashland, Oregon

Book design by Ray Rhamey

Print edition ISBN 978-1-7330344-5-6

Library of Congress Control Number: 2021946930

Dedicated to my husband Dennis,
my soul mate and yoga partner

In memory of Abe, Belle, and Laura,
who are always with me

"My name is Tsoai-talee. I am therefore, Tsoai-talee; therefore I am....The storyteller Pohd-lohk gave me the name Tsoai-talee. He believed that a man's life proceeds from his name, in the way that a river proceeds from its source."

—N. Scott Momaday, *The Name*

"To change, people need to become aware of their sensations and the way that their bodies interact with the world around them. Physical self-awareness is the first step in releasing the tyranny of the past.... To know who we are—to have an identity—we must know (or at least feel that we know) what is and what was 'real.'"

—Bessel van der Kolk, MD, *The Body Keeps the Score: Brain, Mind, and Body in the Healing of Trauma*

Contents

Preface

It is a warm June day in 2002. A soft breeze is coming in through the open windows in the Shadowbrook Room at the Kripalu Yoga Center in Lenox, Massachusetts. With legs anchored, spine extended, arms outstretched, chest open, and gaze focused on a mind empowering warrior II, I catch myself breaking into an involuntary smile when I imagine my parents' reaction to their daughter in training to become a yoga teacher. After all, they upheld the importance of the life of the mind, not the body.

How would I explain to my parents, now deceased, how a late-in-life exposure to yoga brought me to this yoga center and why yoga has such a strong hold on me? This memoir tells that story. At first, I wrote about my struggle with yogic breathing, the beauty of the postures, my first yoga teacher, and how I developed my own yoga practice, but something was missing that would make my story real. When I turned the clock back to traumatic events in my childhood, I instantly knew I had hit on the missing link. What did that memory have to do with yoga? As it turned out—everything.

I was a red diaper baby, a child of parents who were members of the United States Communist Party. My childhood and youth unfolded in the shadow of my parents' all-consuming political involvements during the Cold War era. Shortly before the arrest of Julius and Ethel Rosenberg in the summer of 1950 on suspicion of conspiracy to commit espionage, our family of four disappeared behind the Iron Curtain. Who were my parents? What did they do that sent our family into exile for thirteen years? My parents, Abe and Belle Chapman, worked for the American Communist Party that collaborated with Soviet Intelligence to convert the world to a Communist social system. The roots of my yoga journey go back to the political conflicts I was born into, decades before I knew yoga would be such a transformational force in my life.

My memoir is a story of disintegration, integration, and reconciliation in three parts: my life in exile where Ann became Anička, the remaking of myself back into Ann, and how my yoga journey brought my separate identities together.

Part I:

Vanishing into Exile—From Ann to Anička

"I am thirteen years old, and we are emigrating. It's a notion of such crushing, definitive finality that to me it might as well mean the end of the world."

—Eva Hoffman
Lost in Translation: A Life in a New Language

1: *Going Underground*

One hot summer night when I am eight years old, my family's lives are changed forever. The year is 1950, and my parents are called to a meeting in the Lebanese restaurant Mazzat in downtown Manhattan. This is what I imagine taking place after they enter the restaurant and a man in a suit and tie waves them over to his table in a dark corner.

"Sit down, comrades," the man murmurs without revealing his name. "I already ordered so we're not disturbed." He wipes the sweat off his brow with a folded white handkerchief, then places it in his right breast pocket with care. "Things are heating up."

"There will be serious consequences if they're on to Harry Gold's work on the bomb," Abe says without taking his eyes off their underground contact.

"Since they arrested Fuchs for espionage, they've stepped up surveillance of our activities. There'll be more arrests if they get enough evidence to press charges against David Greenglass."

"Who do you think will be next?" Belle asks with a straight face.

Droplets appear again on the man's forehead. "We're presuming it could be Julius and Ethel Rosenberg."

"That would have serious implications for the work we've been doing," Abe says, keeping his voice low.

Belle scans the tables nearby for possible listeners. Satisfied the other diners are oblivious, she sighs. "Is there time for the Rosenbergs to escape? Their sons are younger than our daughters, eight and twelve."

"We'll do all we can to save them from a public trial. But things are happening faster than predicted."

After a silence, Abe and Belle say in one voice, "Are we in danger?"

The man leans to muffle his voice. "That's why you've been called here."

Belle's and Abe's eyes meet.

"Abe, we expect any day you'll be summoned to appear at the McCarthy hearings."

"They won't have to dig that deep to implicate me. What are my options?" Abe pulls his cigarette pack from his pocket, thumps it on the table until a cigarette falls out, picks it up, and waits for what is coming.

"We've planned an escape for your family. You have a week to get your affairs in order."

Abe waits for this man in the shadows to meet his eyes before asking, "Where will we be going?"

"The documents for your escape behind the Iron Curtain are ready. You'll be living in one of the Eastern Bloc countries." He pats Abe on the shoulder. "Your expertise on Marxism and journalistic skills will be valuable to our Soviet comrades. Staying here could ultimately land you in prison."

The conversation stops as the waiter brings the food and walks away. Pushing his plate aside, the shadow-man says softly, "We all have to make sacrifices for the cause. And getting your family out in time is a priority."

Belle, always practical, squeezes Abe's hand. "When do we leave? And how long do you think we'll be in exile? We need to say goodbye to our families."

The man pulls out his handkerchief, blots his dripping forehead again, then uses it to cover his mouth to mute his tone. "Party orders! Your families must not know you're leaving the country. The FBI will harass your families for leads, so it is best they don't know where you are. And length of time?" He shrugs his shoulders. "Indefinite at this point."

"The FBI?" cries Belle.

"Hush," he admonishes.

Belle grasps Abe's arm. "What about the kids?"

"Trust us," says shadow-man. "The Mexican and Soviet comrades will handle the logistics with great expertise. We're at war, and the enemy is after us. We have to outsmart them."

Belle nods stoically. "We understand. We will comply with the orders." Placing her purse on the table, she signals it is time to leave.

Meeting Belle's stare, shadow-man says, "One last thing. Take no more than two suitcases. *Always* assume you're being watched." Without losing eye contact, he hands her an envelope with train tickets, passports with forged names, and a packet of money she inconspicuously slips into her purse.

"You'll never see me again. Our comrades will be in touch to settle the final details. Keep your departure a secret from your children. To avoid suspicion, they must go to school right up to your disappearance."

"Our apartment? Our things?" Abe asks.

"The Party will pay your rent for as long as necessary to make it look like you're coming back. This will give you plenty of time to get to the Eastern Bloc."

Abe and Belle's food remains untouched. Leaving the man at the table to take care of the bill, they walk toward the door. Exchanging glances, Belle, looking through the glass door for anything suspicious, pauses to readjust her purse on her shoulder. With heads held high, they step into the artificially lit Manhattan streets, not a word spoken between them.

2: *On the Run*

Pooh is snuggled under my arm, and the covers are bunched up around us. Belle shakes my shoulder, whispering, "Ann, wake up." It's still dark outside, so she turns my light on.

"It's shining in my eyes," I complain.

Briskly, she hands me my clothes she must have prepared on the chair while I was sleeping. In a strained voice, she says, "We're leaving in a few minutes. Dress quickly."

Still groggy, I slip my dress over my head, looking over my shoulder to see Laura sitting on the edge of her bed. Her disheveled red hair drapes her partially closed eyes. Struggling with the buttons on her blouse, she gives me a puzzled look.

"No time to linger," my father calls out, peeking his head in the door. I grab Laura's warm hand as I walk toward the door scanning my books, drawings, and dolls scattered around our bedroom. After all, I reason, how long can we be away if my parents only have two small suitcases for the four of us?

Stone-faced and silent, my parents usher Laura and me into a waiting car that looks ominous in the darkness. The driver speeds through the deserted city streets, lips tightly clenched, eyes on the mirror as if we are being followed. *Grand Central*

Station—I sound out the three words on the lit-up sign. The driver pulls up in front of the entrance. The brightly lit lobby is teeming with rushing people carrying suitcases and travel bags. In school, we studied a colony of hundreds of ants that seemed logical, organized, but these throngs of humans— pushing, dashing, all compelled by a voice on the loudspeaker to get from one place to the other—unsettle me.

I turn to my sister four years older than me and wise to the ways of the world. "Laura, where are these people going so late at night?"

Shrugging her shoulders, she brings her finger to her lips to let me know this is no time for questions. I wish I were an ant safely in the colony instead of swallowed in the immensity of the building's structure. The clicking sound of people's shoes rubbing against the marble floor quickens my pace. Abe and Belle take turns looking back every few seconds as if expecting to be approached.

When I stop to admire the lit-up four-faced brass clock in the main concourse, my mother taps me on my shoulder to move me along. My parents direct us toward a platform with a big number eight. "Hurry, hurry, you two!"

When we reach the platform, Abe says with relief, "This is it. This must be our train."

What a coincidence, I think, *platform eight and I just turned eight. Maybe it's a sign something special is going to hap-pen?* And just as I am about to tell my parents about this coin-cidence, the conductor's whistle signals it is time to board. My father picks me up under my armpits to lift me onto the train.

I feel his labored breathing against my neck and perspiration dripping from his face onto my arm.

"That's it. One more step and we're in," he says in a voice I hardly recognize. "In a minute or two, we'll be off." His eyes dart to my mother putting out her cigarette stub with a hurried twist of her right foot before she grabs the railing and swings herself up the steps, practically falling into my father's arms. Their eyes meet, telegraphing success.

Snuggling up against my mother's bony shoulder, I sense this is not the right moment for explanations. I watch the city lights fade and then disappear altogether. Only an occasional glimmer flashes by the window as the train speeds into dense darkness. *Why did my parents keep this trip a secret from Laura and me?* My big sister stares out the window, and the troubled look on her freckled face makes my stomach tighten. Nobody is talking. Oblivious to their ashes falling to the floor, my parents have blank faces. The corners of Abe's mouth are tightly shut. He is rubbing his chin with the middle and index finger of his right hand, which is stained from the unfiltered cigarettes he smokes incessantly. His shoulders are hunched as if he is guarding himself from an invisible danger.

Gone is my mother's smile, which usually lights up her face as if she is embracing life's wonder. With her shoulders rigidly pulled up toward her ears, she looks like it is an effort for her to breathe. Her long, elegant fingers are gripping the handles of her pocketbook, turning the skin around her knuckles white. *If only I could hear her velvety voice, things would be so much better.* Instead, the rhythmic hum of the train's wheels against the tracks brings me back to recent incidents that make me suspicious something strange has been going on.

A few days ago, a small red ball I got from my best friend Ruthie for my birthday rolled across the hall into my parents' bedroom. When I crawled under their bed to see where it landed, I felt two hard boxes. *What?* A large box blocked my view so that I couldn't see the back wall. Curious, I forgot the ball and tried to pull the box out from under the bed. My small hands could not maneuver it.

Still prostrate, I turned around and pushed my feet under the bed, placing one foot on each side of the box. Slowly with my feet, I pushed the box from side to side, inch by inch, until it was halfway out. Stunned, I stopped and jumped to my knees. Instead of a large box, there were two small suitcases under their bed.

Mystified, I dashed into the kitchen. "Are we going someplace? I found two packed suitcases under your bed!"

Usually calm, Belle looked rattled. "Ann, you're old enough to keep a secret, right?"

I nodded enthusiastically.

"We'll tell you all about it, but not now."

I studied the intent look on Belle's face. "But…" I protested.

"Until then, it's our secret." She gave me a conspiratorial glance that made me feel grown-up. "Remember," she said, putting her finger to her lips, "not a word to anybody, even Ruthie." Belle turned to the stove with her lips tightly clasped around her cigarette, making it clear there was nothing more to talk about.

Only a few days ago on my way home from school, a group of my peers were clustered as I walked by; their loud voices and threatening fingers pointing at me made me run. The din became a cacophony. "Commie, get out of here! We don't want you here!" they yelled, shaking their fists in the air. Alarmed at the menacing sound of their voices, I feared they would hurt me. With hands clasped against my ears, I ran up the front steps, pressed hard on the doorknob, and pushed the door open. Shaking, I called to my father, who was lost in thought at his typewriter.

"Abe, Abe!" I yelled, flailing my arms. Like most children of Communists, my sister and I called our parents by their first names, a sign of their radical break from tradition. "Why do these kids hate Communists? Why are they mean to me? What did I do that's so terrible?"

Resting his hand on my shoulder, he reassured me, "They get that hatred from their parents. You see, Ann, America is divided between Communists who want to make the world a better place for everybody and those who don't want those changes to happen."

Relieved, I threw my arms around his waist, letting out a sigh of relief. "I feel better already," I announced as I hopped off to my room thinking he must be very, very wise to write all those articles that got printed in the newspapers and magazines scattered around our living room.

Listening to the radio later that evening, my parents gave each other one of those "This is very serious" looks when they heard the words *Communists* and *arrests*. The hand my mother was using to move the iron along my father's shirt stopped in midair when the name Rosenberg came up. Abe put his arm around her slender shoulders, smoothing out her tightened cheek with a kiss. Hugging my fuzzy Pooh Bear I had gotten for my birthday a few weeks earlier, I felt a tight knot in my stomach. *What changed the atmosphere in the kitchen so suddenly from relaxed chatter to sighs and worried looks?*

And just the other day, I overheard my sister yelling at my mother, "You and Abe are hiding something from us! What do these tense looks and hushed silences mean? Something is not right around here."

"It's just the troubling news on the radio that shook me up," Belle replied in a tired voice.

Now that I am sitting on this train, the secret about our trip is out, but not why we are taking it and where we are going. Desperate for sleep, I lean my head against Belle's chest, synchronizing her shallow breaths with mine. The motion of the train and the surrounding darkness lull me into a fitful sleep.

In Mexico City, we are met by a dark-haired man whose heavily accented English sounds like the words can't get through his thick mustache. He drives us to a secluded house on a residential street while talking about something that brings tight worry lines to my parents' faces. Are we in Mexico City for several days? Weeks? Do I have any toys to play with? Do we eat Mexican food? Am I scared? Listless? Unhappy? Cheerful? My memory of those days is blank, except for aimless strolls through outdoor markets with the smell of fried food and pungent spices, the colorful clothing of drifting crowds, and the melodic sounds of the language. I never forget, however, the loud voices that awaken me from a deep sleep and my mother's shrill voice rising to the second-floor landing, where my sister and I are leaning over the banister to see what the commotion is about.

"Hurry down! A car is waiting! We must leave *right away!*" Belle frantically motions us to come downstairs.

"But I'm still in my nightgown," I call out.

"There's no time to change. Let's get into the car!"

My body swaying from the quick turns of the car, I keep my eyes glued on the driver's hands turning the wheel to navigate the sharp curves in the mountainous roads. My heart sinks as I listen to the fast, clipped English exchange between my father and the driver. The tone of their voices implies we are escaping from some danger, though I can't figure out what that danger is.

"If they arrested Morton Sobell at the Mexican border," my father says, taking a deep breath, "we could be next."

"They'll never find you in these mountains. In a few hours, you'll be safe on the farm," the driver says. I doze off to the vibration of tires rubbing against the uneven pavement. A family with three sons, older than Laura and me, are expecting us at the isolated farmhouse surrounded by a thick stone fence. With limited success, we use hand gestures to communicate. They bring us into a small room off the kitchen, where I collapse on one of the creaky cots in the middle of the sparsely furnished room. There is a wooden statue of Jesus on the wall across from my cot, and his sad eyes make me wonder—is he sad for me, or am I sad for him?

"Is this our new imprisonment? How much longer are we going to be running from place to place?" Laura asks, gasping for air.

My mother strokes her back with even, gentle movements. "Laura, take deep breaths. You'll be okay. The Mexican comrades are looking out for our safety."

Desperate to get her asthmatic breathing under control, Laura follows my pacing father with bloodshot eyes. She presses her hand against her chest each time a wheezing sound is released from her lungs.

My heart beating fast, I watch the frenctic rise and fall of Laura's breathing. In concert, my breath stops and starts in uneven spurts. The more Laura gasps for air, the more my breathing tightens up as if my breath is stuck in the dark chambers in my body. "Will Laura be okay?" slips out of my stiffened lips. Abe and Belle slump on their cots like two stone statues accentuated by the bright moonlight shining through the window. Silence. Flutters in my heart accompany that now familiar pit in my stomach. The pain moves up into my face, landing in my eyes, and tears roll down my cheeks. I'm terrified.

In a lifeless voice, Abe explains, "We'll be here until the comrades decide it's safe for us to continue our journey. Nobody in the village knows we're here. During the day, you'll have to be in this room, but at night you can go into the courtyard for some fresh air if you stay very quiet. But for now, let's get some sleep."

Weeks pass in monotonous sameness.

"Let's count the seven bright stars of the Big Dipper very quietly so the chickens and dogs don't wake up," Laura proposes one night as we're looking up at the sky. "Maybe the stars know why we're here."

Holding back tears, I whimper, "I miss my friends. Ruthie most of all. And Pooh Bear must be wondering where I am. What about the schoolwork I'm missing? What's going to happen to my poem the teacher posted in our class? I can't remember how it went anymore."

Laura's arms wrap around my shivering shoulders and she pulls me toward her. Stroking my hair, she says in a grown-up voice, "Most likely, even Abe and Belle don't know what will happen next. Let's pretend this is a mystery story and we can't know how it ends until we finish the book."

I squeeze my arms around Laura's waist, absorbing the warmth of her thin body. "I like that idea. Do you think this is the beginning of the story or the middle?"

"For now, we don't know, but in time we will," she reassures me.

Every day, I mindlessly copy words from books I do not understand until my hand is too tired to hold the pen. It makes me feel like I am doing big-girl stuff. Jealous of their freedom, I watch the chickens and dogs roam in the dirt-covered courtyard.

"Look how the chickens are fighting to be first at the pail of food," I say one day to Laura. "They're so mean to each other. That one over there grabbed the food right out of the other chicken's mouth."

"Maybe you could write a story about the chickens, and I'll draw the pictures," Laura says, livening up a bit.

"Yes! Let's make it really funny so Abe and Belle will laugh."

Later, in the dark outside the bedroom window, Abe and Belle are smoking in the courtyard.

"Laura, what's going to happen to us?" I ask.

"We're not going home," Laura says in a flat voice.

"How do you know that?"

"The other day, I overheard Abe talking with one of those dark-haired men who visit him late at night. They talked about an American who was caught at the Mexican border. It sounded like some big danger is closing in on us."

"What will happen to us if Abe and Belle go to prison?" I cry out, pulling my blanket to my chin.

"Perhaps we'll get out of this place before something like that happens. Let's imagine what it will be like when we leave this farm."

Closing my eyes, I imagine myself running through a field with colorful wildflowers, my hair blowing in the wind, my arms flapping to the rhythm of my footsteps. My reverie is interrupted by frightening, high-pitched voices coming from the other side of our bedroom wall. The words *FBI, atomic bomb, Soviet Union,* and *espionage ring* sting me with their threatening incomprehensibility. I bury my head in my pillow.

I pretend I am sleeping when Abe and Belle sneak back into the room. Not wanting to worry my sad-looking parents, I stop asking questions and voicing my fears. Instead, I push them away, pretending they do not exist. Here, on this Mexican farm, I learn to suppress feelings I cannot understand or cope with. Later in life, however, those buried feelings return in a most unexpected way.

When we leave the farm, my mother, sister, and I board an airplane that takes us to Holland. My father disappears with no explanation about his whereabouts. A smiling blond stewardess gives me a delicious milk chocolate in the shape of a wooden clog and a coloring book with pictures of windmills and happy people. I trust I am on the way to a fairyland where I will be free to walk outside in broad daylight without fearing for my safety.

3: Behind the Iron Curtain

Straight from the airport, we are whisked off to a cabin on the edge of a thick forest. Each day, Laura grows paler and more lethargic. We see nobody aside from the Dutch comrades who bring us food and warm clothing to supplement our meager summer wardrobe. By now, the trees are shedding their leaves, and the air is crisp and cool. After what feels like a few months, the three of us, disoriented and homeless, board a plane in Amsterdam that lands on a gray, rainy fall day in a country with the letters *P-R-A-H-A R-U-Z-Y-N-Ě* on top of the airport building.

"Where are we?" I ask Belle, who is busy helping the weakened Laura off the plane.

"We're in Prague, Czechoslovakia. We will be here until we're reunited with Abe."

A kind-looking man who speaks very good English drives us to an inconspicuous hotel called Flora off the center of town.

Belle navigates between the hospital, where Laura is being treated for a severe case of hepatitis, and our hotel room, where I spend my days watching the street life from our third-floor window. Forbidden to leave the room, I make up stories about the people coming in and out of the stores with little dogs and small children. Their language is not as melodic as Spanish, and when I try to imitate the sounds rising to my window, I sound more like a croaking bird than the people on the street. The smell of sauerkraut and sausages from the hotel restaurant makes my stomach growl. For hours, I count the white, pale pink, and blue square cobblestones arranged in attractive patterns I so long to walk on.

A few weeks later, Laura is back in the hotel, and I am holding a fork to Laura's mouth begging her to eat just two peas. Uninterested, she turns away, pressing her head into the enormous puffy pillow. My happiness at her return fades quickly.

"Please talk with me. I was so lonely without you."

Instead of answering, she closes her eyes and lets out a long, heavy sigh. I hold Laura's hand, afraid that if I let it go, she might disappear again.

The next day, she calls me over to her bed. "What did you do while I was away?"

"I watched people from the window and made up stories about them. I saw a lot of tiny dogs that look like hot dogs with short legs and mothers with net bags filled with groceries. The kids bring home pitchers of beer from the pub on the corner. Some of them lick the white foam on the top of the pitcher. And they carry their milk in tin cans. Everything is different here."

Months pass. Our solitary life changes with one phone call.

Shaking with excitement, Belle yells into the receiver, "Abe! Is that really you? Where are you?"

I hear my father's booming voice through the telephone receiver. "I'm in Prague!"

"Where?"

"The Alcron Hotel on Štěpánská."

Our reunion is loud and joyful. Abe gives us delicious chocolates in shiny papers called *mishki* ("little bear" in Russian) along with pictures of Moscow's massive buildings, wide boulevards, and subway stations with enormous statues and tile pictures of soldiers with guns over their shoulders, happy peasants with rakes and bundles of wheat, and smiling workers on an assembly line.

With dreamy excitement in his eyes, he tells us stories about the wonders of the Soviet Union, where he spent the last few months. "Both your mother and I thought we would be settling in the Soviet Union. But the comrades decided our home will be here, in Prague."

When things calm down, my parents call me over for a "serious talk."

"In a few days, we'll be moving to an apartment in a neighborhood called Kobylisy where you'll be attending school. Before we can move out of this hotel, your name will have to be changed."

"Why can't I be what I already am?" I ask.

"In order to live in this country, you will be Anna Čapková," Abe says, as if giving me a compliment. Belle lets Abe do all the talking while she studies the pattern on the carpet.

I look at them, dismayed. "But I've always been Ann Chapman," I say.

"You must forget you ever had the name Chapman." Waiting for this to sink in, Abe gives me a serious look. My face has gone blank, as has my brain. "Anna Čapková. Repeat after me, Anna Čapková." Abe smiles as I let these sounds slip off my tongue, sounds that are meant to erase Ann Chapman from existence.

To accompany my linguistic efforts, Belle waves her hand like a musician with a baton. Čapková, Čapková, Čapková. I repeat it like a code that will release me from months of stifling confinement.

"You got it. That's it," she says with an encouraging smile.

"And Laura will also be Čapková?" I ask in a wavering voice.

"Yes, she'll be Lora Čapková. It's a fresh start in a new country. This is the new you."

Abe smiles while I experiment with finding the voice that will sound most like me when introducing myself as Anna Čapková.

Finally, we have a home of our own on a quiet street with mature trees and a carefully tended garden behind a wooden fence. The two-story villa has leafy vines creeping up its outer walls. Beyond a metal gate, a cement pathway leads to this early twentieth-century villa that once, I am told, housed the Zapletal family and a maid. Miss Zapletalová, the sister of the previous owners, lives on the ground floor. The Schneider family occupies the first-floor apartment. We live on the floor above them in a two-bedroom apartment. There is a basement with cubbies for coal for the kitchen stove and storage bins for a winter's supply of potatoes. A big washtub with a scrubbing board is for laundry, which is carried in baskets three flights up to the attic to dry.

Inside our apartment, four doors open off a long, uncarpeted hallway. The first to the left is the toilet, separate from the bathroom with a sink and tub. The big glass doors to the right lead into the living-dining room. The kitchen at the end of the hall has a small balcony overlooking the garden immaculately tended by Miss Zapletalová. You enter the bedrooms from the living room. The one to the right is for my parents, and the one on the left is for Laura and me. Our bedroom shares a wall with the kitchen where my parents, and their frequent visitors and friends, talk late into the night around the kitchen table in voices significantly happier than in Mexico.

This sunny apartment is furnished with what the previous owners left behind. The ornate white bureau and beds with a golden finish are nothing like the simple furniture in our Bronx home. One night while horsing around, Laura and I accidentally dislocate the painting behind her bed, and to our shock, discover a metal safe built into the wall. Despite our heroic efforts, our hairpins cannot open it.

Later, our parents explain that the previous owner, Mr. Zapletal, was a pilot who worked for the RAF. When the Communists took over, he escaped with his wife and two daughters to England hours before the borders were closed. Ironically, by the time the safe was opened, the large sums of money from the previous regime were no more valuable than toy money!

I quickly fall in love with the neighborhood where I come to know every alley and secret pathway, go sledding down a nearby hill, walk to school, shop in the local stores (especially the bakery with crusty rolls and rye bread), and visit the neighborhood library up the hill. In later years, I learn that every house tells a unique story about what happened to peoples' lives after 1948 when the Communists came into power. These single-family houses were broken into multi-apartment dwellings without any concern for the property rights of their owners. For me, ignorant of the brutal history that preceded my arrival on Nad Rokoskou street number 39, these are the best years of my childhood.

The principal of my elementary school, Comrade Kotková, is a short, middle-aged woman with a kind face and soft voice. She takes me by the hand to bring me to my classroom with a big 4A posted on the door. Pushing and shoving to get closer to this strange creature who appeared in their midst, the kids shout out names I can't pronounce: Bohuslav, Václav, Jiří, Sáša, Jiřina…

My mispronunciations amuse them. Pointing to me, they want to know my name. Nervous I do not accidently revert to my aborted name, I pronounce each letter with great care: "Anna, Anna Čapková."

They giggle, shaking their heads no. They call out cheerfully, "Anička, Andulka, Anča." Amused at my bewilderment, they nod with playful vigor, adding once more, "Anna ne," and raise their arms to indicate it is the name used for grown-ups.

Once again pointing to me, they repeat, "Anička? Andulka? Anča?" and lower their hand to my height.

I nod in agreement. "Anička," I say, pointing my finger to the middle of my chest. "Anička. Okay?"

"*Ano, ano* [yes, yes], Anička." They clap to show I got it right.

Without a choice in the matter, and too young to understand the future ramifications of my name and citizenship change, I wholeheartedly plunge into acquiring all that would make Anna Čapková real: mastery of the Czech language, membership in the Pioneer Organization, love for Father Stalin, an ardent trust in the power of the collective, and an enthusiasm for building a bright Communist future. Discarded, and ultimately forgotten, is the name Chapman, never again spoken in our home, and with it, the person Ann Chapman used to be.

4: *Language Defines Who I Am*

Learning Czech, of little interest to my parents, is my only means of escape from the isolation I have lived in since I walked out of our Bronx home. My first Czech lessons take place on the walk to and from school, on the playground, and when playing street games with the neighborhood kids. Pointing to a house, they have me repeat *to je dům, kniha, sešit, péro, učitelka, kamarádka* (this is a house, book, notebook, pen, teacher, friend), correcting me until I get the pronunciation right. I repeat these words while washing dishes or walking to the grocery store until I have them memorized.

One day, a young teacher with a disarming smile and a head full of unruly chestnut-colored curls, Comrade Svobodová, approaches me in the hall and says, "Stop by my class after school." When I do, she directs a long wooden pointer to a chart with a maze of words with interchangeable endings. "This is how Czech grammar works," she says in a decisive voice. "You'll have to learn these endings to speak like a Czech. This is how we say 'I love bread with butter': *Já miluju chleba s máslem.* But 'You love bread and butter' is *Ty miluješ chleba a máslo.*"

I throw my arms in the air, despairing at the magnitude of this task.

"That's not all," she adds. "Each noun is masculine, feminine, or neuter, and the endings change accordingly."

"It will be years before I make a sentence right with all those endings."

"Aničko, take it step by step. To get started, memorize this list of endings, and read these poems out loud every day," she says, handing me *Mateřídouška,* a magazine with pictures of smiling Pioneers (the Communist version of Scouts) on the cover. "Next week, come to my home with a notebook and pen. My mother will make *poppy koláče* [filled pastries] we'll have when we get our work done," she adds, handing me a paper with her address.

I race home, and as soon as I'm through the door, I yell, "Belle! Did you know the Czechs are the smartest people on earth? How else could they create such a complicated language?"

That night before falling asleep, I repeat *kniha* (book), *s knihou* (with a book), *v knize* (in the book), and *koláč, koláče* until sleep silences my voice.

After months of intense immersion and plenty of frustration sweetened with home-baked goodies, the efforts of Comrade Svobodová and my teacher-classmates usher me into the Czech-speaking world. Soon I am reading, writing, counting, speaking, thinking, and dreaming in Czech.

"Ann, you can't say *I never don't not want* in English," my frustrated mother corrects me.

"Why not? The Czechs do it."

"Double negatives work in Czech, but we never use them in English."

"Why don't you learn some Czech?"

"Why do you refuse to read in English?" she snaps back, pointing at the shelves of English books in my father's study.

From this day on, I use Czech with everybody except Abe and Belle and their foreign friends, thus splitting my world into two estranged compartments. The more my Czech vocabulary grows, my English vocabulary stagnates. A passionate reader, I refuse to read in English despite my parents' consternation. I love what words convey and how they fire my imagination.

Once a week, I climb the hill to the neighborhood library for a fresh supply of Soviet socialist realist novels and Czech classics. From the former, I absorb the ideology and values of a young Communist who devotes her talents to the common good. Meanwhile, from the Czech stories and myths, I get a feel for the rich history of this age-old people.

"Good to see you, Aničko," the librarian says, reaching under her desk. "I put aside a few novels I thought you would enjoy."

"I finished all three volumes of *Far From Moscow*," I tell her. "I want to be like Vasili Azhayev, who worked in the outposts of Russia."

"Your time will come to help build Communism. Meanwhile, keep reading and studying," she says, stamping my stack of books.

"I bet I'll find new friends in these books," I say, swinging my packed schoolbag over my shoulder and heading home.

Music, a world without words, is the language that unifies our family. In the elegant Prague concert halls with plush red velvet seats and golden chandeliers from the pre-Communist era, music transcends our conflicts over the use of English, Czech, and double negatives.

The mournful folk tunes of the Red Army Chorus send shivers down my spine, and the Moiseyev dancers twirling to heartwarming folk tunes transport me to a world of movement and sound where words are unimportant. Dvořák, Smetana, Chaykovsky, and Mussorgsky all open me to the world of feeling beyond words and sustain our familial bond beyond the concert halls.

One evening, we sit scattered around our living room: Laura is drawing in her sketchbook; Belle, Abe, and I are reading. Abe puts on a record, and turning to me, he says, "Ann, listen closely. This Bach Cello Suite no. 2 is Laura's favorite." He looks at her, his hand across his heart, eyes half closed, body swaying to the warm cello sounds. "Can you *feel* that beauty? Really, really feel it?" He looks at me with moist eyes.

Unexpectedly, the deep cello sounds tap into a longing for what I left behind to become Anička. Fuzzy memories assault me, the music converts my longing into a sadness, and my arms and legs are weights. I can't feel them, I can't move them. Laura's hand stops moving. Belle raises her head, takes her glasses off, and rubs her eyes. Moving his head in harmony with the music, Abe pulls us into Bach's world, satisfied that music has summoned profound and exclusively positive emotions.

As Czech, a language that excites me, attains a flourish and subtle nuance of expression, English no longer does. Through reading, writing, and daily relating, my Czech is in a constant state of growth. English, a necessity in my home with non-Czech-speaking parents, is divorced from the Czech life that has come to define who I am. At the core of my Czech selfhood is its language that expresses my deepest thoughts and feelings as no other language can.

5: My New Family

With a happy trill in her voice, my friend Božena announces, "We're going to Vysoký Chlumec to see my grandparents who live on a farm. My grandmother lets me get the eggs out of the chicken coop for her *bábovka* [pound cake]. I'll bring you a piece when I get back."

"I'd love that. My mother doesn't bake that much."

"Did your grandmother bake?"

My mind wanders to my grandparents' kosher home with my grandfather praying in Hebrew in a hypnotic monotone and my grandmother handing me a slice of fresh-baked challah. "Ann, come set the table. Be sure to use the *milichdick* [dairy] silverware because we're having blintzes," my grandmother instructs, the aroma of homemade soup drifting through the house. Her voice is calm, soothing. Her white hair pulled back in a bun, she's wearing a white blouse with a golden pendant that glows when the sun shines on it.

Božena interrupts my memory flash. "Aničko, what are you thinking about? You never answered my question."

"It's been so long, but yes, she baked wonderful bread, and..." An upwelling of longing sends a spasm through my cramped stomach. To change the subject, I dare her. "Who'll be first down this hill?"

The moment is gone. Erased. Obliterated. Expunged.

Abe's Communist loyalties mean all contact with relatives in the States is *forbidden*. No phone calls. No letters. No photographs to remind Laura and me of our American families. The Chapman and Shulman families no longer exist in my parents' narratives.

My father, Abraham Chapman, the fifth of six children, was born in Chicago in 1915 to Tzvi and Chassie, religious Jews and avid Zionists. Witnessing violent street riots between Jews and Arabs when visiting his married sister in Tel Aviv, Palestine, radicalized him to fight for the underprivileged at an early age. Instead of completing his college education, he joined the Communist Party. Under a variety of aliases, he wrote for Communist publications like the *Daily Worker* and *New Masses,* and he taught Marxism at the Communist-sponsored Jefferson School.

My mother, Isabelle Shulman, was born in 1915 in New York City on the Lower East Side to Orthodox parents who were also fervent Zionists. She embraced my father's conviction that Communism was the answer to correcting the world's ills. To a young woman who scorned the subservient role of the female in the practice of Orthodox Judaism, Abe offered a way out. He was everything she was looking for: Jewish, intellectual, and charismatic. He also offered direction, inspiration, and an intoxicating goal toward a promising future. He soon became the man she loved.

Abe and Belle met in Palestine and married, at age eighteen, in an Orthodox wedding in Tel Aviv in 1934. They settled in New York City, which, at the time, was the hub of social and political radicalism. Synagogue services were replaced by peace marches and political rallies defying segregation laws. Relations with their families were secondary to furthering the Communist cause. The final rift with their families was solidified when they vanished from their lives during their thirteen-year exile in Czechoslovakia and China—and in place of their original families, they embraced the larger Communist family.

These people who live and travel throughout the Communist Bloc are, for the duration of our stay in Prague, my substitute family as well. Though they are not blood relatives, they are a source of colorful history and stories that give a sense of continuity and belonging. They bring a purposeful intensity and vitality into our home along with a sense of shared camaraderie. They appear and disappear on an unpredictable timetable. They are subservient to Party orders, and their frenetic and complex personal lives resemble those of spy-thriller characters. Some have permanent jobs in one of the Communist countries; others live under assumed names and identities while working for the underground network. In the warmth of our family circle, they cling to an illusory sense of a close-knit family they were exiled from in their own families.

They shower me with attention, love, chocolates wrapped in shiny papers, fancy boxes of cookies, much-valued chewing gum, Pete Seeger and Weaver records, and sometimes a sweater or blouse from the "forbidden" West. They praise my mother's kugels and soups made on our coal stove while passionately debating the Party's struggle against "US imperialism and its war machine."

Ken and Irving are my favorites. Ken, whose real name is Harvey, spends many hours in heated debates with Abe, his guru on the teachings of Marx and Engels. He works in one of the Communist Youth organizations that has its headquarters in Prague.

"Marx was right about the alienation of the masses in a capitalist society. The socialist system will change that," Abe states with unshakeable conviction as Ken takes notes in his little notepad.

Then Ken says, "Here are my questions from my latest readings of *Das Capital*. Are you ready?"

Abe listens before launching into long, complicated answers that make no sense to me. This leads to more questions and hours of discussion. While I work on my homework at the dining room table, their excited English-speaking voices form a rhythmic background to the Czech sentences filling the pages of my school notebooks.

Ken joins our family when he is twenty-six and I am thirteen. He likes to tease me. "Let's see how good your math is. When I'm twenty-seven, you'll be fourteen. Will I still be twice as old as you?" He is fun, energetic, and interested in what is going on in my little world. He has a smile in his eyes before he gets to the punch line of a joke, and his unruly curly black hair makes him look like a playful koala. In addition to spending long hours discussing ideological issues with Abe, his mentor, he cooks with Belle, makes hot chocolate for me, tells funny stories about his New York childhood, joins us on hikes in the outskirts of Prague, and jokes around with Laura. And then one day, he disappears into the Communist void.

My mother puts my persistent questioning about his disappearance to a close. "Ken isn't coming back to Prague. All I can tell you is that he's safe and doing good work for the Party."

Thus Ken slips out of my life, and I don't know if I will ever see him again. My heart shrivels the way it did when I left my best friend Ruthie in New York. It will take years for the ache of this loss to recede.

Irving Potash is older than Ken. He is distinguished-looking with silvery hair and a measured, calm manner. The twinkle in his pale blue eyes suggests life is one big amusing game, and that he is up for it. He always makes time to take long neighborhood walks with me or go over the schoolwork I translate into English. In conversations, he looks straight at me as if nothing else matters. He surprises me with an unexpected visit when I am in Pioneer Camp some one hundred kilometers from Prague. Briefly, I harbor the illusion of having a grandfather, perhaps not a blood-related one, but a deeply heartfelt one. Irving's funny facial expressions and wild hand gestures bypass the need for a translator when relating to my amused campmates. That sweltering hot day, when I proudly show him around my camp on Lužnice River near Tábor, is the highlight of my summer.

During his visits to our Prague apartment, Irving captivates us with stories from his prison days. "The criminals and the political prisoners are mixed in together," he starts explaining. Then, with a devilish sparkle in his eyes, he takes me by surprise when he asks, "Annie, do you want to know how we outwitted the rats in our cell?"

"Weren't you afraid of them?"

"We got them to fear us. We saved bread we shaped into hard balls we used as bullets. When hit, they scrammed into the other cells. They were smart enough to know our cell was a deadly war zone," he laughs good-naturedly.

Curious, I ask, "Were the criminals horrible people?"

"They wanted to know why we were Communists and what we did that got us into jail. Until this day, I'm proud of converting some of the criminals to Communism!" he says with a tinge of incredulity in his voice.

Irving is also a high-ranking Party functionary and an organizer for the Furrier Union. Whenever I enter the room, my parents' hushed voices, no doubt discussing Irving's secret activities, come to a halt. From his travels through the Eastern Bloc, he brings us jars of black caviar from the Soviet Union, kashkaval cheese from Bulgaria, juicy sausages from East Germany, and halva [a sesame paste candy] from Poland.

"Irving hasn't seen his daughter for several years. If he goes back to the States, they'll arrest him. Though she's older, you remind him of her," Belle says one day, letting me into a small part of Irving's mysterious life. And though he never talks about his family, and I never ask, just knowing he cannot see his daughter makes me feel we have something important in common—a desire for a relationship that would make up for our absent families. We enjoy our closeness that has no past history and an unpredictable future.

After a particularly long disappearance, he shows up with a bushy moustache.

"Belle," I confide, "I hate Irving's moustache. It doesn't look like him."

"Why don't you tell Irving?" she prods with a perplexing gleam in her eyes.

"I can't do that. It will hurt his feelings."

"I don't think so." She pushes me gently in his direction as soon as we reenter the living room.

"Ann has something to tell you," Belle announces.

"This moustache doesn't look like you. I like you better without it," I mutter.

To my surprise, he roars heartily. "You know what? I also don't like it. One day, your mother will tell you why I have it. For now, you must forgive me for looking like this. I haven't changed. I'm still the same Irving." He pulls me toward him for a tight bear hug.

That is the last time I see Irving in our Prague home.

Shortly after this visit I learn from Belle that Irving was arrested in New York City. He'd grown that moustache to return to the US on urgent Party business. Still, they recognized him and caught him anyway.

I am shattered with grief.

With no continuity or predictability in my relationships, I never know if those I have come to love will disappear for good or inexplicably reappear. It leaves me longing for a stability and certainty that does not exist in our exile behind the Iron Curtain.

6: Reinventing Myself

The lights are out in our bedroom.

"Well, Mrs. Dvořáková," I address my sister in Czech, "I was lucky to find a piece of beef to make a goulash. But the potatoes were old and shriveled." Playing the role of Mrs. Nováková, I imitate her grown-up voice.

"I only got six eggs after waiting online for half an hour, enough to bake *buchty* [yeast rolls filled with poppy seeds or jam]. My kids will be thrilled," my sister, now Mrs. Dvořáková, says in a comic voice before bursting into laughter.

On another night, Laura starts up in the serious voice of her teacher, Comrade Nosek. "Today we're discussing Jirásek's *Ancient Bohemian Legends*. Lora, could you please read the opening paragraph of the tale set in Old Prague on page fifty-six?"

I immediately counter that by becoming my teacher, Comrade Kotková. "Please copy these sentences," I say, pointing to an imaginary blackboard, "and then convert them into the past and future tense. Watch out for irregular verbs."

Night after night, Laura and I practice our Czech through the voices of our neighbors, teachers, friends, and local shopkeepers by reenacting what is happening in our daily lives. From now on, our English-speaking parents cannot penetrate our secret language and the world that goes along with it.

The big day I impatiently awaited is finally here. Belle is ironing my white shirt and navy-blue skirt while I rehearse the pledge I will be reciting at my initiation ceremony into the Young Pioneer Organization. "I, Čapková Anna," I say in a serious voice, "am joining the ranks of the Vladimir Ilyich Lenin All-Union Pioneer Organization, in the presence of my comrades solemnly promise to passionately love and cherish my Motherland, to live as the great Lenin bade us to as the Communist Party teaches us to as required by the laws of the Pioneers of the Czechoslovak nation and our President Gottwald."

Though Belle has no idea what I just said, she looks pleased. "Your voice is sincere and strong. You'll be an exemplary Pioneer!"

My chest puffed out, I place my right hand in front of my forehead for the pioneer salute. "I'm as ready as I'll ever be," I say, reaching for my crisply ironed clothes.

The four of us take tram 11 to the House of Pioneers. People are pouring into an imposing building with marble pillars at the top of the staircase. Exalted, I step into the auditorium decorated with Czech red, white, and blue flags and Soviet red flags, which show a golden hammer and sickle with a single star. Banners with slogans like "A Pioneer is an example to all, Always forward, not a step back" crowd the walls. Barely able to contain my excitement, I join my Pioneer troop backstage, where our leader gives us last-minute instructions on how to properly walk on stage.

My posture proud, head high, eyes aglow, I walk up the steps to the podium where the dignitaries are waiting to greet us. Aware my parents are watching, I recite my pledge with conviction and feeling. Saluting the commander, whose chest is covered with distinguished medals, I call out the salute, "Always ready!" to which he responds, "Be ready!"

Ceremoniously, he ties a soft red scarf around my neck. When reunited with my family, I say proudly, "From now on, I'm not only Anička—I'm a Pioneer!" *And now I am like everybody else!* I think happily as we make our way home for a celebratory meal.

On May 1, International Workers' Day, I march with my Pioneer troop across town with my home address pinned to the inside of my skirt in case I get lost. We end at the main square, Václavské Náměstí, where we are greeted by president Novotný. I scream, "With the Soviet Union forever! Lenin lived, Lenin lives, Lenin will live!" and "Workers of the world unite!" with the cheering crowds until I lose my voice. Zealously, I wave the Czech and Soviet flags to the tempo of blasting military bands. My heart beats wildly at the sight of the president dressed in a dark suit flanked by Party dignitaries in military uniforms. They salute from an elevated podium decorated with photographs of model workers who overfulfilled the projected plan for their unit. Swept up in the excitement, we chant in unison:

"The people and the Party are one."

"Didn't these blisters hurt you?" Belle cries out later when bandaging my feet with tender care after I have limped my way home and up the stairs to our apartment. I reply, as a brave Pioneer who has walked more than fifteen kilometers should, "I had more important things to pay attention to than some insignificant blisters."

I run home from Eva's house pressing the box of sweet-smelling Christmas cookies to my chest like a box of fragile eggs. "Eva's mother gave strict instructions," I announce, removing my coat and boots in the doorway. "We're not to eat them until Christmas Eve. That's the tradition," I say, using the tone of voice my teacher uses when she wants to get our attention.

Belle admires their beautiful shapes, commenting, "They smell so good!"

"These are the vanilla crescents, and those over there are bear paws, and the ones with jam are called *línecké koláče!*" I explain enthusiastically to the uninitiated. I point to an empty place under the living room window. "Can't we have a tree this year? This is such a perfect spot."

"Jews *don't* celebrate Christmas." Belle's voice wavers. "We celebrate Hanukkah."

"That's what we did in New York. But I want to be like my friends. We haven't had a Hanukkah celebration since we came, so why not do Christmas instead?" I persist. "They're selling Christmas trees at the Kobylisy market. And they have big wooden barrels with live carp for the Christmas Eve dinner. Can't we *please* at least get a carp?"

Belle's resistance dampens my enthusiasm. "Who wants a live carp taking up residence in our bathtub? Besides, I don't know how to cook it."

In a few days, Abe surprises us with a small Christmas tree, a box of shiny glass decorations, and clip-on holders for candles. Laura squeals with delight when she unwraps the box of smiling elves with pointy hats and red mushrooms with big white dots. Meanwhile, my mother disappears in the kitchen.

"Give her time to adjust." Abe winks conspiratorially like a five-year-old kid. "A Christmas tree is not part of our family traditions, but these are unusual circumstances."

Laura and I nod. We call out in high-pitched voices as we decorate, "Here, over here, this branch needs something. And the star goes on the top!" Pulling Belle out of the kitchen, I show her what we did.

Still looking sad but not angry, she says, "Okay, but this is it. No carp. At least not this year." Her lips stretch into the beginnings of a smile.

Establishing a new family tradition, Abe puts on Jakub Ryba's eighteenth-century Christmas Mass. The sugar-coated bear paw cookies from Eva's mother—a mixture of butter, flour, ground nuts, cocoa, cinnamon, and cloves—melt in my mouth.

The next year, a live carp shows up in our bathtub. While humming a Christmas carol, I take a sponge bath in the sink, keeping an eye on the carp splashing around the tub. *Are we really going to eat you? It's so much more fun having you in the tub.*

"Well, Abe, it's time," Belle says, handing him a big kitchen knife.

"How should I do it?" he says, looking at the carp apologetically.

Laura and I close our eyes. Nothing happens. Belle takes the knife out of Abe's useless hand and with one swift stroke brings the carp's life to an end. My father covers his eyes before Belle slices the carp's head off. Triumphant, Belle pronounces, "Here it is, ready to go in the pan." Abe looks at her with admiration. Her attempt to make the traditional black sauce with prunes, raisins, walnuts, and wine smells better than it tastes, but the potato salad is excellent. That is the first, and last, Christmas that Belle allows a live carp into our home.

As our Jewish and American holidays fade into the background, Czech Christmas, Easter, and Pioneer activities eradicate the already fragile link to my previous American identity. I am, however, unaware of a huge disruption that is about to threaten the Czech identity I established in what was once a land of strangers but is now my home.

7: A Major Upheaval

Abe's booming voice resonates through the house. "China is the future! Not like Stalin, Mao has it right!" To prove it, he shows us pictures of the great Chairman Mao waving to thousands of people in drab blue outfits on Tiananmen Square. "How do you like the Peking opera?" he asks of the record he is playing.

The disharmonious sounds grate on my ears, but I smile politely, trying not to dampen his enthusiasm.

"Mao's campaign to let a hundred flowers bloom and a hundred schools of thought contend is rippling through China at lightning speed," Abe explains as he spreads the gifts he brought back from his three-month stay in China.

I am drawn to the fragrant scent of jasmine tea, exotic spices, weird-tasting gooey candies, and lychee fruit with their bumpy light-brown shells. My eyes feast on the ivory chopsticks with engraved Chinese characters and delicate blue bowls with translucent designs. There are colorful silky brocades with pagodas and unintelligible Chinese characters, cave rubbings of bamboo trees and horses on soft rice paper, and scrolls with paintings of mountains disappearing in the clouds and water buffalo plowing through rice paddies. "Let me teach you how to use them," Abe offers when he notices I am examining the Chinese characters on a pair of smooth ivory chopsticks. "And this over here," he says, reaching for a tea-green jade pendant, "is for you."

Abe ceremoniously clears his throat and gives us a meaningful look. "Your mother and I," he announces, lovingly wrapping his arm around Belle's narrow waist and meeting her radiant gaze, "have been offered jobs in China."

"Jobs?" Laura says in a mistrustful voice. My body goes on alert; my heart is in my throat, my fingers curl into fists, and my head pounds.

"I'll be editing the magazine *Peking Review*. Belle will be working at the Foreign Language Press."

Screechy sounds of Peking opera camouflage the unsettling silence.

Abe waves his lit cigarette in the air. "We'll be off to Peking in a matter of weeks. These are such exciting times in China," he says as if already on his way toward this new adventure.

Laura and I exchange a look that says *Oh no, what about us?* My stomach clamps up. My heart sinks. Devastated to leave the life it took years to establish, I dread having to start over with a new language and culture. At the same time, I am curious about life in an exotic place like China.

Laura's shrill voice breaks through my jumbled thoughts. She makes a stab at defending our interests. "You expect me to disrupt my university studies? And what about Ann's studies at the gymnasium?"

My voice trapped in my chest, I let Laura do the talking.

"I can't face another upheaval," Laura cries.

"The Chinese comrades will work out the details of your education. What a unique opportunity to experience a thousand-year-old culture and the revolutionary changes that are taking place."

In my state of shock, the unintelligible words from Abe's record sound like a falsetto forewarning of a dislocated future.

In the year 1958, when I am not quite sixteen, the Trans-Siberian train takes us through the thick forests of the Siberian steppes past the ocean-sized Lake Baikal, the Mongolian steppes with grazing cattle, mountains bathed in golden sunlight, and miles and miles of Chinese rice paddies with water buffalo like those pictured on the scrolls Abe brought back from China. On the sixth day, the train arrives in Peking to cool, sunny weather.

The car taking us from the train station competes for space with crowds of black-haired people dressed alike and fearless rickshaws weaving through heavy traffic. We are assigned a small two-bedroom apartment in the Foreign Language Compound. Nothing is familiar: my pillow is as hard as a rock, and the refrigerator is a wooden box that gets refilled with big blocks of ice delivered by a man with a horse-pulled wagon. I watch from my bedroom window how toddlers squat to pee on the street through a slit in their pants to bypass wearing diapers. The market near our compound is teeming with people bargaining for fruits and vegetables I cannot name in a language that sounds like an atonal musical composition.

Laura moves into a dorm at Peking University to study the Chinese language and history, and I attend a Chinese school where the only class I can follow is midday gymnastics. Trying to master thousands of Chinese characters and four tones that distinguish one word from another is like climbing Mount Everest.

At the height of my frustration, I charge into my parents' bedroom. "How do you expect me to get on with my studies when I can't understand what they're saying? Even that old man in a long black robe and beard teaching me to write Chinese characters can't speak a word of English. I want to go back to my school in Prague!" I collapse on their bed in tears.

This outburst gets me transferred to a Russian school on the outskirts of Peking in a compound called Druzhba (Friendship) built for Russian families of scientists and technicians working to advance the Chinese economy. I dress like a Soviet schoolgirl in a dark-brown dress with a white collar and black apron, and my name is Anya; gone is Czech Anička. As I launch an intense campaign to study Russian, I am relieved it at least belongs to the Slavic family of languages like Czech. I fall in love with the beauty of the Russian language and its writers: Turgenev, Gogol, Chekhov, Pushkin, Lermontov, and above all, Tolstoy. The nineteenth-century characters in their novels and stories loom large in my imagination. Their loves, disappointments, and deliberations about how best to live their lives weave in and out of my dreams.

Near the end of our second year, the "blooming of a hundred flowers" turns into a reign of political terror. Exploration of opposing views that initially attracted Abe and Belle to the Chinese version of Communism is being brutally suppressed. By 1960, the Chinese Communist Party promotes an anti-foreigner campaign that threatens the personal safety of fellow travelers like my parents. Their ideals shattered, my parents escape on the Trans-Siberian train and avoid the fate of their Communist friends who stay behind—imprisonment.

Prague! I immediately pick up where I left off two years ago. I cram two years of material for my gymnasium exams to graduate with my class and start my studies in the humanities program at Charles University. As a trilingual oral translator for the Czechoslovak Communist Youth organization, I travel around the country with foreign delegations, fully aware that the way the Party representatives present life in Communist Czechoslovakia is riddled with falsehoods. Since I'm cut off from contact with Western countries, this is the only life I know and the only place where I feel at home. Little do I suspect that the major upheaval I just lived through was merely a minor preview of what is to come.

8: *My World Collapses Again*

Gypsy melodies wrench my heart as I descend into the depths of Prague's catacombs. The flickering candlelight on the tables creates a warm atmosphere in the smoke-filled wine cellar. Seated at a table adorned with a red and white hand-woven table runner, Bohouš waves me over. Pretending to hold a violin, he moves his imaginary bow and taps his foot, laughing. We kiss. Pointing to barrels of Moravian tap wine, he asks in a voice that makes me weak in the knees, "Red or white?" After our jug of wine and platter of Slovak goat cheese, Moravian sausages, and dark crusty bread arrive, Bohouš picks up his glass.

"To our love." His shiny dark eyes behind his stylish, black-rimmed glasses gaze lovingly into mine.

"I brought you a surprise. Can you guess what it is?" I pull the latest issue of *Plamen* (*Flame,* an exciting literary magazine) out of my bag. "It has Kundera's 'Love' poems. Let me read you this one." I turn the page to the poem I like most. Bohouš lights my cigarette. My voice slow and sensual, I look up every once in a while to gaze into his glowing eyes. His big, warm hand cradles mine.

"Just one more kiss," he pleads as I wrap my arms around his neck in the darkened hallway of my Vinohrady apartment building.

"See you at the university coffee shop," I whisper, snuggling into his arms.

"I'll let you know how I like the poems," he says on his way toward the door.

Being careful not to wake my parents, I unlock the door to our apartment. At the threshold to the living room, I stop short. *What are they doing up at such a late hour? Is it Abe's heart again?*

"Ann," Abe sings out in a youthful voice, "we've been waiting up for you. We have very exciting news! We'll be returning to the States once our identities and names are restored. It will take months and will involve lots of paperwork." He points to a stack of documents on the coffee table.

Thunderstruck, I reach for the nearest chair. The effect of the wine instantly evaporates, as does the security I felt in Bohouš's arms a few minutes ago.

"We're happy we will be returning home. Abe's recent heart attack was a terrible scare, but there's hope we can have a new start," Belle says, invigorated by having months of anxiety over Abe's precarious health behind her.

Watching their joy, I am torn between protecting Abe's fragile health and admitting my devastation.

"Abe! Is this for real? How can you do this to me?"

"Ann, calm down, let me explain," Abe says, stretching his hand in my direction.

My body as tight as a bow, my feet unsteady, I inch toward the door as I scream, "Leave me alone!"

In my bedroom, I collapse on my bed. Words elude me. *Can I withstand so much grief?* I pull my blanket over my head and squeeze my knees into my chest, rocking softly from side to side.

A few days later, my parents ask me to join them in their bedroom. I have hardly spoken to them since I learned our lives in Czechoslovakia are nearing an end. Abe is sitting in bed propped up on pillows, eyes half-closed. Pale and worn, her mouth clenched and eyes restlessly darting around the room, Belle is seated at the foot of their bed.

I pace back and forth, shifting my gaze from my mother to my father. "You wanted to talk with me?" I say in a flat voice. Silence. Making sure our conversation doesn't get out of hand, I say warily, "In my wildest dreams, I never believed this would happen."

"Ann, please get settled. Give us a chance to explain." My mother casts a worried look at my father. "We must clear this tension. We're all suffering."

In a grave voice, Abe defends their decision. "We never expected to live here our entire lives. America is our home." He closes his eyes to recoup his waning energy.

Slumping into the nearest chair, I say, "You're forcing me to leave what is my home. I'm not the eight-year-old you pulled out of America. I'm twenty-one with a life of my own! I feel no connection to the States. None. My life *is* here: my studies, translating jobs, relationships, Bohouš." I look away, too distressed to continue.

Getting hold of Belle's hand, Abe says with a cracking voice, "It's our responsibility to bring you back to the country of your birth." He looks in my flaming eyes for signs of understanding.

Belle wipes the sweat from his forehead with a handkerchief. "We *desperately* want to rebuild our lives in America before Abe has another setback."

An eternity passes. My voice shaking, I cry out, "Will I always be an extension of your lives?"

Belle looks pained. "We can't undo the past. We plan to leave the Party as soon as we get back. We have to follow Party orders until our return." The impasse remains: their salvation is my doom.

Pained by our conflicting needs, Abe says in a barely audible whisper, "America is where we all belong. I can understand you don't see it that way *now,* but that will change in time. You have your whole life ahead of you."

I start pacing again, then shout, "America is *your* home, not mine." I squeeze the statement out of my lungs as if it is a mournful tune coming out of an injured accordion. "Because of your commitment to Communism, I am firmly rooted in this place!"

Across the room, I hear my father's heavy breathing. Belle's eyes narrow slightly but remain dry.

"Furthermore, you made me believe the life I was living as Anna Čapková was not a temporary stage performance with a surprise ending." Crippled by sorrow, I slide back into my chair, my head dropped between my slumped shoulders. "This place is embedded in the core of my being," I say without any hope it will alter my predicament. I feel like crying—no, I feel like shouting. I do neither. Speechless, I shift my weight to the back of the chair.

"Unless your American citizenship is reinstated, you'll be stateless," Abe says, leaning back on his pillow, his eyes misty, his knuckles white from gripping Belle's hand.

"This has already taken too much out of us. There's really nothing left to say," I say.

"Let's leave it for now," my mother says. "Your father needs to rest. It rips us apart to see you suffering like this." Her shoulders trembling, she wraps her arms around me.

Crushed, I turn in the doorway. "How did it ever come to this?" I blurt.

On a crisp September day, Laura and I take a farewell walk through Prague before we take off for different countries on separate continents. Arm in arm, we stride along the embankment of the Vltava River with the view of the Prague castle in the distance. My heart breaking, I glance at the Gothic steeples of Saint Vitus Cathedral, a landmark of Prague's long history. I turn to Laura, her face a reflection of her conflicting emotions: she is eager to join her Czech husband Pavel, who has a teaching appointment in the Asian Studies department in Cambridge, and at the same time, she is dreading our impending separation. Tears streaming down our faces, we know our lives will never be the same. She is starting her married life in England, a country she knows nothing about, and I, against my will, am off to return to America. Our family will be separated by the Atlantic Ocean with no date of a reunion in sight.

"Take a picture of me right here so I can remember this moment, this day, this city, this life," I say, wiping a tear off Laura's cheek with my thumb. "This place will always be home for the two of us."

"Whatever happens, you'll always be my baby sister," she says, putting her arm around me the way she used to when we were small.

9: *Returning to America*

Numb, I watch the passengers on the SS *France* ocean liner laugh, dance, and drink the night away. My heart shriveled into a hard ball, I wonder if I will ever again be carefree and happy like the people around me. On a cool, gray morning, the ocean liner circles the Statue of Liberty, a symbol of freedom and a fresh start for millions of immigrants and exiles. Not for me. I cling to what I left behind, dreading the implausible future. Straining to see the skyscrapers shrouded in fog, I press my hand to my palpitating heart. Is this how Abe felt when he had his heart attack? Or is my heart breaking in two?

The ocean liner docks in the harbor. A crowd waving bouquets of flowers shouts, "Abe and Belle are here! They're back!" as the three of us make our way down the gangplank. An explosion of hugs, kisses, and cheers accentuates the grief flooding my heart.

Their voices breaking with emotion, my parents call out, "Kate, Moe, Stanley, Betty, Ira, Esther..." as they hug and kiss their friends who stayed behind. No relatives are here to welcome us, only my parents' old friends and comrades, all strangers. This moment marks the end of my parents' exile and the beginning of mine.

Everything about New York City is intimidating. Its cacophony of sounds, long avenues, blinking neon signs. The
continuous sirens of police cars and fire trucks. The stench of
hamburgers, popcorn, and hot dogs. Where are the narrow
medieval streets with Gothic church steeples, Baroque palaces,
cobblestone sidewalks, houses with centuries-old frescoes, and
yellow trams snaking their way through the winding streets?

Postscript

Irving Potash, clean-shaven and with a few more gray hairs
than I remembered, unexpectedly shows up at our Manhattan hotel. Though his prison term is over, he still works for the
Party. My parents' exile over, they are in the process of severing their relationship with the Party. After hugs and tears of
joy subside, Irving puts his finger in front of his closed lips and
points to the walls. He pulls out a yellow legal pad, on which
he writes in big letters: *This room is bugged. We must write.*
Leaving the Party after twenty-five years means Abe and Belle
can no longer keep up a personal relationship with people like
Irving. You are either in or out of this tight circle of believers;
you are either trusted or a traitor. This carefully orchestrated
reunion is not a resumption of our relationship but a final and
deeply painful parting.

"Abe!" A man with slumped shoulders in a woolen plaid blazer
and fedora runs up when we exit through the gate in Chicago's
O'Hare airport. "Is this you?" he wraps his arms around Abe's

shoulders, pressing him to his chest. "My baby brother! I never thought I'd see you again. No letters or phone calls! The family didn't know if you were dead or alive. If only Mama had lived long enough..." His voice cracks. "Belle," he says as he moves over to give her a hug. "And this must be Ann? What a young lady. Welcome to the family. Welcome to Chicago." He steps closer, unsure if he should shake my hand or hug me.

"This is my older brother, Nate," Abe says when he collects himself. I look for some resemblance to my father to be sure this stranger is my uncle.

"We're off to Adele's house. The family is anxious to meet you."

A long ride later, Nate pulls into Adele's driveway, and children peer out a window of the house, screaming, "They're here!" Another crowd tumbles out the door laughing, crying, and shouting all at the same time. They pass Abe from one set of arms to another as if they need to convince themselves it is really him. When the excitement reaches a more manageable level, they turn their attention to Belle and me. I know Abe had five siblings and that Manny, Fanny, and Belle are no longer alive, and neither are his parents, but I never realized how many cousins, nieces, and nephews he has.

"Ann looks just like our sister Belle, don't you think? Amazing!" They study my facial features, oohing and aahing as if I were an exotic creature from another planet. Questions like "Ann, what are you planning to study? How do you feel about being back?" only exacerbate my misplacement. I have no plans. I have no direction. I have no home. And I feel no connection to these strangers. I feel shut out of my parents' lives when they tell stories about Rhine, the husband of Abe's sister Fanny, a great poet and intellect who never regained his mental powers after being hit by a car. It is painful to realize they have past histories with these people I know nothing about.

At the dinner table, weighted down with chicken soup and matzo balls, challah, platters of brisket, kugels, and salads, they share stories about deceased family members as if they were still here. I find it unnatural to call these people aunt, uncle, or cousin, words that had till then had no place in my vocabulary.

Longing for her company, I write Laura a long, heart-wrenching letter about my first impressions of America and the Chapman family reunion. I conclude, "I don't belong here. My body is here, but I'm not. You were so fortunate to be spared meeting the family, because it only confirmed what misfits we are."

We are visiting old friends of my parents in the Bronx. My mother is dialing a number from a piece of paper with a shaking hand. In a voice strained to the breaking point, she says, "Papa, this is your daughter Belle." Within seconds, sobbing hysterically, she crumples on the stool under the wall phone. Her shoulders shaking violently, she is unaware the receiver slipped off her lap. Her grief, hidden from me for the duration of our exile, is unleashed.

"What happened? What, what did your father say?" Abe asks, wrapping his arms around her trembling body.

Barely audible, she repeats her father's words: *I have no daughter.* She folds into Abe's arms. With a pained expression,

Abe rocks her, smoothing his hand across her wet cheeks. Pure, unstoppable pain shakes her curled-up body. Seeing her pain and vulnerability softens the resentment of my own loss. Tears streaming down my face, I join Abe and Belle in a silent knot, each needing the warmth of our love to be felt and known.

Belle reestablishes a fragile relationship with her mother and brother, but her father never gets beyond the hurt of having a daughter who defied everything that was sacred to him.

Abe and Belle start the process of rebuilding a life as private citizens. Everything is a struggle—finding jobs with unconventional resumes, reestablishing relations with family, and stretching their limited finances. But toughest of all is what we avoided talking about in our family of four: crashed ideals and disillusionment with a political system to which they sacrificed so much, and which altered the course of their daughters' lives.

Everyday life in America is an endless challenge: shopping (after a lifetime of shortages, I can't handle so many choices), banking (overwhelming), advertising (intrusive), casual conversations (no politics please!). The adjustments range from the ridiculous to the crucial: getting used to the American tendency to smile all the time, learning to drive a car, and groping my way to defining a future for myself. Longing to be back in the life I navigated so easily, I am dependent on others to coach me through the practicalities and subtle differences of American life.

Abe shifts his focus in his writing and teaching from the political arena to literature and the arts. Belle gets her driver's license at age fifty-two (after failing the test four times) and her BA at age fifty-four. She is a librarian in a Catholic high school in the small town of Stevens Point, Wisconsin, with pictures of Jesus on the walls instead of Marx and Lenin. Always the stabilizing force in the family, she keeps the household running while Abe cranks out articles and books that put him in touch with a wide circle of poets, writers, and journalists. But for Belle, it is a rocky road back to normalcy that very few can understand. No one even knows about the action-packed life she left behind. "Just imagine how many countries I could have been imprisoned in if they only knew what I know," she blurts one day with no further explanation. Is it a joke, truth, or fabrication? With Belle you can never be sure, though I suspect there is some truth to it, but how much or what that truth is never gets clarified.

Abe writes his poem "I Climbed the Moonbeams of Desire" in the intensive care unit when his heart is giving out. It explains what he could never talk about with me face to face:

> I climbed the moonbeams of desire
> In the midnight of misty quests,
> Mind's midnight dawns of hope and expectation.
> And slid down the solid sun rays of raw reality,
> In the noons of unslacked shadows
> And parched shadows of the sun-drenched day
> and darker than the shadows of the night,
> The midnight dawns of quests and questioning
> in the answerless sunlight

Of reality unfathomed
Wander lust
Wander lost
Wonder lost

I understand the opening line, "I climbed the moon-beams of desire," to be a reference to his crumbled dream, whereas in the line "The midnight dawns of quests and questioning/in the answerless sunlight/Of reality unfathomed," he reveals the elusive nature of his quest for answers and understanding. Returning to his homeland with an ailing heart and shattered faith in the vision of a better world, he is not ready to give up on life. Literature gives him what politics robs from him—faith in man's ability to transform himself. After a life of *Wander lust/Wander lost/Wonder lost*, he settles for the "raw reality" of what life is and not what he dreamed it could be. No longer the all-knowing guru, he is the seeker who must slide "down the solid sun rays of raw reality" before he can land back on earth.

I fumble through my early months in the States in a hazy fog without direction or goals. I am granted a Ford Foundation Fellowship in the Slavic Studies graduate program at the University of Chicago, where I major in Russian literature (my life-long love) and minor in Slavic linguistics and Czech literature. While my classmates struggle with their Russian, something I excel in, I cannot spell or write in acceptable English. I go through the motions of getting through my classes estranged from myself and those around me. They know nothing about the world I am coming from, and I am clueless about theirs.

I lack a shared point of reference with my American peers and the background to penetrate the perplexity of American life. I like the songs of Hegerová and Eva Pilarová and contemporary Czech and Russian authors; they talk about films, TV programs, books, and singers that mean nothing to me. Because I was raised to focus on the importance of the collective, the American emphasis on individualism is foreign to me.

In search of answers, I immerse myself in nineteenth-century Russian literature. Lev Tolstoy, firm about his moral code and beliefs, becomes my mentor the way Abe was for Ken as I search for a value system to live by. But isolated in an amorphous void, my absorption in Tolstoy does not yield the hoped-for result—a way out of my confusion.

I meet my future husband, Dennis, in the Slavic department at Cornell where I am hired as a teaching assistant of Russian and Czech. His second-generation Slavic background is a good fit with my Czech past. He speaks several Slavic languages and plays folk songs on his accordion that remind me of singing along in Prague wine cellars and pubs. The birth of our son defines my new role—a giver of life. My identity as a mother is without the ambiguity I feel in my American life. My baby and I are defining our lives: one with an identity yet unformed, the other still formulating one. Motherhood brings me a purpose and stability I never thought possible after what I lived through during our exile.

10: *Abandoned*

Despite Abe's failing health, Abe and Belle drive from Stevens Point, Wisconsin, to Binghamton, New York, for a Passover Seder with their grandsons Daniel and Michael, aged five and two.

Dressed in a suit and tie at the head of the table, Abe uses his strong voice to guide Daniel through the four questions: Why is matza eaten on this night? Why do we eat maror (bitter herbs)? Why do we eat meat that has been roasted? Why is food dipped twice in salt water? We pass around the Passover platter with the symbolic foods to be reminded of the story of the Jews' escape to freedom. Daniel never takes his eyes off Abe's animated face, while baby Michael plays with the shank bone on the Passover platter, unaware of the importance of this event. For the grandparents and grandchildren, this is a successful celebration; for me it creates a troubling dilemma that dates to our family history.

Belle and Dennis volunteer to put the kids to bed while Abe and I go for a walk. The evening sky is like an abstract painting of soft grays and blues in a background of floating pale gray clouds.

"That was such a nice celebration," Abe says as we turn the first corner. "Daniel was so interested in the Passover story. Did you see the Passover pictures we made this afternoon?"

"Yes. Very nice."

"You don't sound like you mean that."

"Of course I do."

"But?"

"I'm not sure this is the right moment." I pause. "Why go into our past?"

"What exactly do you mean?"

"Well…but why spoil the good mood?"

Fighting the sadness welling up in me I turn my attention to the patches of melting snow next to the crocus shoots and miniscule buds on the forsythia bushes. Abe's voice breaks through my thoughts.

"If something is bothering you, let's have it."

"The truth is, I have no feeling for this holiday."

"No feeling?"

"Why should I pass it on to my children if it has no meaning for me?"

"All you need to do is read a few books to catch up on what you missed."

"You can't be serious."

"It's a matter of attitude."

"Feeling for a religious holiday comes from experiencing it firsthand. After all, it's not an intellectual pursuit. It has to come from the heart."

"I never thought it would be this hurtful for you."

"I didn't want to get into it."

"I'm glad it's out in the open. Is there any way I can make it easier?"

"Next time, ask me how I feel about bringing that holiday into my home. Between Dennis's Orthodox holidays, my Czech holidays, and your desire to resurrect the Jewish holidays we missed out on, where is the real me in all of this?"

"I should have been more sensitive to your feelings. We don't share the same past, though I wish we did. Can you forgive me?"

The tightness in my shoulders dissipates. I breathe in the vibrant spring air and with it a wave of excitement pushes away my dark feelings.

"Taking your classes on American literature helped me better understand the American part of you," I say with a voice gaining in warmth. "Your Jewish roots are still somewhat of a mystery. I'm afraid it might be too late to change that. My roots are more Czech than Jewish, though I do love it when you sing those Jewish folk songs," I say, wrapping my arms around his shoulders in a tight hug.

My arm intertwined with his, we walk back to the apartment building in a comfortable, contemplative silence.

Smiling, Belle looks up from the newspaper. "The kids are fast asleep. They sure loved that bath. How about a nightcap?"

Abe and I in one voice: "What a great idea!"

A year and a half after this visit, the phone rings during dinner. My mother prepares me for the worst. "Ann, your father might not make it through the night. This time, his heart failure is fatal. Come as soon as you can."

The tears come instantly, streaming down my face. Feeling feverish, I throw some clothes in a bag and I call Dennis. "The unthinkable is happening. Abe's dying. Come home." Now shivering uncontrollably, I curl up on the couch; sensing something is not right, the kids play quietly until Dennis gets home to take charge of things.

On the flight to Stevens Point, I remember those late-night discussions about the American writers he loved, he with a bourbon and water, me with a scotch and soda and the cigarette that is now off-limits to him. The list was impressive: Faulkner, Hemingway, Thomas Wolfe, Carson McCullers, Ralph Ellison, Langston Hughes, Saul Bellow, Bernard Malamud, and his beloved poet Walt Whitman. "American literature tells the story of immigrants who remade themselves in America. The same will happen to you if you let it," he said during one of those discussions. "Reading these writers will give you a feel for what makes this country unique."

His eyes fired up, he recited Walt Whitman's poem "Song of Myself" and swung his arms to the rhythm of the words that rolled off his tongue like a bird's love call to his mate: "I celebrate myself, and sing myself,/And what I assume you shall assume,/ For every atom belonging to me as good belongs to you."

Wiping away my tears, I pull myself back into the reality that there will be no more conversations like this, a reality softened now by gratitude that he inspired me to read American literature under his guidance.

When I enter Abe's room in the intensive care unit, I can see in his eyes he knows the end is close. His strong voice is silenced by the tubes keeping him alive, but I reach for his warm hand. How can I transmit my energy to his fading heart? How can he die when there is still so much living to be done? I feel like screaming *He's only sixty years old! And all that knowledge and mental energy—where will it go?*

What can I possibly say in this life-altering moment? The melancholy melody of the Moravian song *Rožnovské Hodiny* finds its way out of my compressed lungs. Stroking his hand, I sing softly: "The Rožnov church bells ring sadly/I am separating from my beloved/though separating we will not part." Sadness welling up in me, this song momentarily bridges the split between our two very different cultures. Abe nods understandingly, his face soft, loving.

A tender squeeze from his hand tells me what I need to know: "I love you, Ann. Nothing else matters." His breathing becomes slower and slower, but my love for him stronger than ever, I am reassured our love has survived the hurt of our differences.

Deep in REM sleep at 3:00 a.m., I am startled by the harsh ring of the phone in our Plattsburgh home. "Mrs. Kimmage?" a woman's voice inquires.

"Yes, that's me."

"Is somebody with you?"

"My husband is here," I answer, tensing against what I know will come next.

"I have sad news. I'm sorry to tell you your mother just passed away."

"Oh, no. No." My body shaking, I fall into Dennis's arms. Anticipating her death for months but unprepared for it nevertheless, my heart quickens its beats.

The nurse's voice brings me back. "Do you want us to leave her body in her room so you can say your last goodbyes?"

"I, we, yes, yes, we will be there as soon as we can…" I trip over my words.

The magnitude of my loss slowly sinks in. Gone with her is my entire history, her bright presence, her charm of a master storyteller, her caring attention, her loving gaze. For Belle, cancer was not a battle; it was as much a part of life as anything else.

As sick as she was, she never lost her flair for the unexpected and unpredictable. With terminal ovarian cancer, she moved to live with us in Plattsburgh with a crate of matzo ball mixes in case they were not available in the North Country. She let her grandsons parade around in the wig she wore after she lost her hair. She showed up at my house in a brand-new car after hesitating to buy a new brassiere when she had so little time left to wear it out. Weakened by chemo treatments, she crossed the Atlantic to see Laura. Over the three-year period of her life in Plattsburgh, she made enough friends to fill the Unitarian church where we hold her memorial service.

I am clearing out Belle's apartment, a job I have been avoiding for weeks. Feeling like an intruder, I start with her desk drawers and find a collection of black-and-white photographs I don't remember ever seeing. There is a photograph of our family in Prague, dressed up and smiling on the day of Laura's eighteenth birthday—Abe in his familiar fedora hat and Belle in her signature gray suit. Laura's dress and my skirt were made from traditional Czech blueprint material we loved. For a split moment, I imagine myself as that fourteen-year-old on an outing with her family.

I pick up a pen and paper to write about the first memory that comes to me: the night Laura and I discovered a metal vault behind a painting in our Prague bedroom. We tried in vain to open it with our hairpins. Night after night, we made up stories about the secrets hidden in that vault.

In a few months, I fill two notebooks with random stories from that stage of my life. Then one day, I write about the vault my parents built to guard the truth about their political activities. I relive my pain at being excluded from having this important key to my life. All at once, I see where this writing is leading me. If I am ever to integrate my past with who I am now, I must separate my story from theirs so I am not bound by their secrets for the rest of my life. And for that to happen, I must let that story unfold the way I experienced it.

I must shake off their taboo of silence and pick open my own locked-up vault where, throughout my childhood and adolescence, I stored the secrets about my true identity. In retrieving my own story, I release pent-up feelings of sadness, confusion, and abandonment. I never imagined the dire consequences my memoir, *An Un-American Childhood,* which started

in Belle's vacant apartment, will have on my relationship with
Laura, Dennis, and ultimately myself.

11: *Trapped*

It is 8:00 p.m. American time and 1:00 a.m. English time when my phone rings.

"How could you do this to us?" Laura screams into the phone. "*You're* writing a memoir? *Our* life? *Our* story? Jeopardizing *our* safety! *Our* past is a taboo subject! And I want it to stay that way!"

"Shedding the secrecy that has been exacted from us is crucial for repossessing my story," I yell, shaken by the severity of this sudden attack.

Silence. Only the sound of Laura's frantic breathing. My mind jams. My heart thumps in my ears. Struggling to steady my equilibrium, I keep my voice down. "Okay, our parents hid their secrets and lived by Party orders. But that was then. It's been thirty years since we left that Communist world. What our parents did is ancient history."

"Fine. Scream it from the rooftops. Our parents' fanatical faith in a false idol wrecked our lives."

I plead for empathy. "Why should I live the rest of my life hostage to their narrative? Breaking that bond starts with *this* memoir. It's no accident the title is *An Un-American Childhood*. An identity lost, not once, but twice. I must salvage those losses so I can incorporate them into my current life instead of burying them. And writing is my way of doing it."

"All I want is to live in obscurity. I'll never trust authorities after what we've been through. Besides, our parents insisted on our silence! Why would you want to relive that past? Why not let it rest for good?"

"Keeping up this vow of silence is deadly poison."

Through her heavy breathing, she yells, "Go ahead, write. But do it for yourself if you need it that badly. But leave the public out of it. Who needs the story of our messy past?"

"I'm entitled to figure out my own story enmeshed in theirs. Think of all those other kids we knew in the Communist circles. My story could help them repossess their own. Besides, what was politics then is history now."

"You *are* betraying us, period."

Her words piercing through me like a sharp sword, I crumple on the chair under the wall phone. Meanwhile, her razor-sharp voice continues, so unlike the loving sister I revere.

"Paul wants nothing to do with you. Nothing!"

"He's your husband—of course he supports you."

"Ann, if you go through with this book, you leave us no choice but to *consider* severing our relationship. This is tearing me apart. You're my baby sister I've loved and protected, and now this." Her words dissolve in sobs.

"Are you content living the rest of your life in the shadow of Abe and Belle's conspiracies? Writing is my way of putting the scattered puzzle pieces back together, a fresh start, perhaps, or a chance to reconstruct a *new*, and more real, me."

Through the phone, I feel her struggle between fury and hurt. "Psychobabble justification. Betrayal is betrayal," Laura shouts, slamming the phone down.

The receiver dangles in my hand long after Laura's raging voice is reduced to a monotonous buzz. Cold, shivering, I cry out into the mute phone, "Laura, our past has us both *trapped*. We must not let it destroy the genuine love we have for each other."

Part II:

Flying Blind in a Land Without Borders

"When body, breath, and awareness are aligned, a certain kind of magic happens. Distraction falls away and all of you comes together into a greater whole. The posture not only stretches you in just the right place, it teaches you something about yourself."

—Yoganand Michael Carroll, taken from *Kripalu Yoga: A Guide to Practice On and Off the Mat* by Richard Faulds

12: There's Always Yoga

Walking early-morning laps around the field house, I am troubled by the storm my memoir has brought into my life. After a sleepless night, my mind is sluggish and my spirits are at an all-time low. I go over and over last night's conversation with Dennis and still draw a blank as to the way forward.

"Ever since you came home from the Hedgebrook writers' colony, you seem distant," he told me. "Is it the absorption in your book, or the new people you're meeting through your research that's pulling you away from me? The book has taken over your life. When was our last hike? Or bike ride with a picnic lunch?"

I tried to explain how the writing is pulling me into Abe and Belle's world and resurrecting the Anna Čapková I used to be. "I feel like I'm on the verge of a deeper understanding, but I never quite get there. So frustrating. I'm in it too deep to stop. It's not that I don't want to be with you. I just can't seem to let go."

Dennis was puzzled. "Is the book that important to you?" he wondered. "Must you put yourself through this? And what about all those sleepless nights about the rift between you and Laura?"

"I have to make sense of what I lived through."

"But what will do that?"

"Maybe digging deep enough to understand and do something to get through this phase of uncertainty."

"Well, I hope it's not too much longer before you get to the finish line so we can get back to some 'normal' living."

"The last thing I want is for this book to affect our relationship."

"Only you can decide what will help you through this. For my part, I'll be happy to have my old Ann back."

I hug my old friend Margo, who gives me a concerned look when we settle with our cappuccinos. "Thanks for coming on such short notice."

"What's going on? You sounded really upset."

"My memoir is turning into a monster. My sister is apoplectic about going public with our story, and Dennis feels I'm wrapped up in my parents' world, which is distancing me from him. Am I right or wrong to keep on writing?"

Margo says in a thoughtful voice, "It looks like writing this memoir has opened a can of worms for all three of you." She stirs her coffee, then adds, "Remember, there are always other ways of dealing with your anguish."

"What do you mean, other ways?"

"There's always yoga."

"You can't be serious! What on earth would yoga have to do with resolving my situation?"

"Remember my divorce?" she says with a meaningful look. "Yoga restored my self-worth. Yoga, like a compass, could help you figure out your priorities."

Not wanting to disappoint Margo, I stay vague. "I can't promise anything, but I'll think about it."

On the drive home, doubts cloud my thinking: *How can some random arm and leg movements get me out of the pain I'm in?*

I reach for the door of the Plattsburgh State Fitness Center aerobics room, then drop my hand. *Should I go in? Should I run?*

Fighting back my doubts, I decide I have nothing to lose and step into the great unknown.

Fifteen people on colored mats are either stretching quietly or sitting with their eyes closed in a spacious, sunlit room waiting for class to begin. Under a large painting of a red cardinal, the Plattsburgh State mascot, a small, bald man sits cross-legged in what I take as a meditative pose. His back is ramrod straight, and his hands rest on his knees with thumbs and second fingers touching, palms facing upward. He wears white baggy pants and a loose-fitting white shirt, and his eyes are closed. The fluffy strip of thin black hair on the back of his head coupled with his delicate features make him look like a bird.

I smile thanks to a young man with a bushy black beard who approaches me with a spongy blue aerobics mat. I'm still wondering whether I should stay or leave when the teacher's soft voice chanting "Ohm" gets my attention. *Ohm?* I wonder. *What's this?*

"I'm Antonio," he says as if he heard my thought. "If this is your first time here, welcome."

Turning red, I lower my eyes toward the floor. *Okay, Margo,*
I say to myself instead, *it's time to prove yoga's healing powers.*

The class begins with a "centering." Sitting cross-legged
with hands resting on my knees and spine erect alerts me to
my tight shoulders and a spine that would rather slump than
sit straight. In an unrushed, pleasing voice, Antonio guides
us into a practice. "Take a deep inhale through your nose. Let
your belly balloon out. On an inhale, bring the breath to the
top of your chest. On a slow exhale, release any remaining tension."

Release tension? He must be kidding. Each attempt to
breathe in this yogic manner tenses me like a tightened screw.
I'm horrified to realize how erratic my breathing is and that my
muscles are as tight as leather.

"Use these deep yogic breaths to support you in the postures," Antonio encourages.

I panic. *I'm running out of steam. I'm a breathing flop.*

The warm-ups make me think of the Tin Man in *The
Wizard of Oz* who needs to lubricate his rusty joints to keep
going. *If only I had his oil can!* When we go into yoga postures with names like warrior, triangle, tree, and sun salutation, my movements are reticent and shaky. In the twelve-
movement sun salutation flow, I can't get my leg to swing
up between my hands from a lunge. In desperation, I look at
the student next to me to figure out what I am doing wrong.
Meanwhile, the students have moved into the next posture
while I am still crawling around my short, slippery aerobics
mat like an ant.

They are getting ready to go into something called tree. I place one foot against the opposite thigh, but within seconds my leg slides down toward the floor. A tree? I can't even manage a mini bush. Thinking I am too old to move my fifty-seven-year-old body this way, I notice, to my dismay, we still have a half hour of class time left. *What was my friend Margo thinking? I'm not made for this. Please, get me out of here!*

I wobble my way into warrior I with one leg lunged forward and arms like wet noodles dangling over my head. Distracted by an unpleasant tremble in the muscles of my extended leg, I forget to breathe through my nose. Instead, I open my mouth to gulp in a fresh supply of air, certain I will suffocate if I keep my mouth closed another second. I confuse my right leg and arm with the left, and vice versa. My movements are fitful, my muscles resistant, my mind a blasting orchestra of discordant sounds. *What a disaster!*

It's music to my ears when Antonio finally says, "Get ready for the last posture of the class called deep relaxation." I collapse into a heap on the aerobics mat as his calming voice floats through the room. "Surrender. Let go. Relax."

Okay, I think, *how do I do that with a tight chest, rag-doll legs and arms, and gasping, ragged breathing?* Irritated, I glance at my watch, though I am supposed to have my eyes closed. Only three minutes left to this agony. Hurrah!

Disappointed, I return the aerobics mat to the closet, and on the way out, to be polite, I say, "Thanks, Antonio." He smiles and nods. Back in the hallway, I edge through the crowd, certain I will not be returning to another yoga class anytime soon, if ever.

What made me want to run instead of embrace yoga the way Margo has? The question keeps running through my head in a loop. True, moving my body forward, back, up, down, and side to side makes me feel awkward and uncoordinated. There is no way my breath will make it through my intercostals to my upper chest for that inaccessible yogic breath. I despair at how hopelessly out of touch I am with my body. *What is so special about yoga, anyway? Then again, why do all these people look like they're enjoying themselves? Is there something wrong with them or with me?*

"How was the yoga?" Dennis asks at dinnertime.

"Awful. The regulars were focused, calm, and graceful. I was everything I am not supposed to be—tense, distracted, and annoyed with my uncooperative body. And the breathing—don't even ask."

"Sounds like you're thinking of quitting. It's not like you, not to give it a chance."

"Margo cautioned me to give it at least three classes before I make up my mind. Should I trust she knows what she's talking about?"

A week later, despite my mental resistance, my body takes me across campus toward the fitness center. The thought that yoga might have stirred something inexplicable flashes through my already agitated mind like a warning: it is time to face the divisions and discord that are getting me down.

13: Breathe In, Breathe Out

A few weeks later, bathed in bright sunlight, the aerobics room invites me in. Young to middle-aged people are resting on their mats or stretching their arms and legs with slow, mindful movements. I take a spot by the glass doors to be close to the lush green meadow. The floor-to-ceiling mirror shows my sad, drawn face. *Is this the way I look when my guard is down? What's buried under this sadness and emotional exhaustion?* My questions unanswered, Antonio's soft-spoken voice brings me back to the aerobics room.

Today, instead of rushing into the postures, I observe first, then practice, then repeat. This was my process when learning Czech, and it worked. Why not apply it to the mastery of yoga? When I diligently follow Antonio's cues for moving my hips and spine, I notice a pleasant sensation in my lower spine that elevates my spirits when I stretch one arm toward the ceiling and an unexpected aliveness when I pull my clasped hands behind my back. With my head below my heart in a calming forward bend, the fog in my head clears as if erased clean. These observations alert me to what is different about yoga and a workout in the gym: by monitoring what I feel as I go into the movements, I involve both the physical and mental parts of the experience.

Each time I alter the position of my body, I feel like a flower awakened from its sleep: a stretch in the back of my legs when bending forward is like the ring of an alarm; an opening in my lower spine when I pull my knees into my chest feels like an inchworm's spinal arch; a pleasant release in my hips when I sway my bent knees side to side opens my chest cavity and hips like an accordion. Just like when I twirl in a foxtrot or glide down a snow-covered hill, my body communicates its likes and dislikes with tireless persistence.

Getting my breath to harmonize with my sensory movements is an ongoing battle. How do I get my mind, body, and breath, each in its solitary orbit, to become a unified team? It should be so simple. We breathe from the moment of birth until the life force leaves the body. We hold our breath when surprised, stop breathing when frightened, enjoy a long exhale when letting go of sadness or tension, and breathe rapidly when excited or uptight. Breath is life, and how I live is reflected in the texture of my breath. Unlike gestures that visibly reveal my inner state with a shrug of the shoulder, a tilt of the head, a piercing gaze, or an illuminating facial expression, breath is intimate, almost confessional.

So why, despite my vigorous efforts, does that deep yogic breath continue to elude me?

"Antonio?" I call out as he heads toward the aerobics room door. "How do you make those deep yogic breaths? However hard I try, I can't do it."

He pulls up his sweater so I can see his belly expand to the size of a balloon on a deep inhale. Pointing to his belly with his index finger, he says, "It's this easy." On an exhale, his belly returns to its normal size. I stare in awe at the rise and fall of his abdomen as if watching a magic trick whose secret I can't figure out.

"That's all there is to it," he says, pulling down his sweater.

"So why can't I do it?"

"Babies naturally breathe through their bellies. That's also how we breathe when we do yoga. However, when frightened, anxious, or stressed, *we constrict our breath* in self-defense."

The dots connect. How I breathe reflects how I feel and live.

"Will I ever unlearn my habitual shallow breathing?"

"Have faith in your body to unlearn old behavior patterns. Don't force it. It will come in its own time." He pats my shoulder in a fatherly fashion as we head toward the door.

Later that day, Antonio's explanation about how the breath is altered by fear and anxiety resonates. Mind flash: I'm on a tree-lined path in a park in the Bronx. I am seven years old. On this warm, sunny day, my parents, absorbed in a discussion about something serious, are strolling ahead of my sister and me.

Chasing after butterflies and birds, I break into a fast run, my arms flapping to the tempo of my moving legs. "Laura, catch me!" My breaths are natural, effortless. I breathe in and out with no struggle, no resistance. There is only a fearless trust my breath knows what to do. Each breath, deeper and more satisfying, flows with the same natural ease of the stream beside me. Smiling, I run toward a tall tree and wrap my arms around its trunk. I wait for my rapid heartbeats to slow down. Again and again, I breathe in, breathe out, singing along with the birds skipping from branch to branch. I wave to my parents, who smile back.

How can I bring those unrestrained deep breaths back into my body?

Like a hypnotizing mantra, Antonio intones, "Breathe in, breathe out. Breathe in, breathe out." More dots are connected when I recall my breath tightening when watching Laura gasp for air during an asthma attack on the Mexican farm. Antonio's clarification that "fear changes the way we breathe" is something I have experienced without making the important connection between my emotions and my breath.

Months pass. My struggle with my resistant breath continues.

It is a beautiful sunny day when I enter the aerobics room for Antonio's noontime class. After teaching two academic classes myself, I am glad to recoup my energy on my yoga mat. Before closing my eyes for a centering, I focus on the image of a strong oak tree in the middle of the meadow. A forceful release in my chest cavity followed by a sweet, unrushed breath ripples through me from the depths of my belly to my upper chest. *How did this much-desired breakthrough sneak in through the back door?* Overcome with gratitude, I greet that breath with the elation of a traveler who completed a triumphant voyage across a stormy ocean. "Here you are! I don't know how you got here but *welcome, welcome, welcome!*"

Antonio is right. Change is possible, even at the age of fifty-seven. Mastery of that effortless, deep yogic breath strengthens my reverence for yoga's power to make change happen. With my breath as my ally, I am ready to write the next of my yoga story.

14: *Yoga Is My X-Ray Machine*

Class is almost over. It is time for deep relaxation or what Antonio calls corpse pose. "Close your eyes. Lie on your back, legs shoulder distance apart, arms forty-five degrees from your body palms up, feet dropped to the side. Align your head with your spine. Let go of any willful holding. Surrender."

As I try to be the corpse I am told to be, something is not quite right. I am held hostage by a sorrow pressing against the walls of my chest the way barnacles cling to a rock. An uninvited memory pierces through me like the spear of a stingray followed by a burst of tears:

Dressed in our best clothes, our family of four is on our way to Prague's American Embassy. Ushered into a large room, we are greeted by a young man in a fashionable suit and tie. He gets right down to business, his voice stern but polite. "We can issue you one-way passage back to the States but not an American passport," he says, looking dismissively at my father as he slides a stack of documents in front of my stone-faced parents. A large American flag behind his desk makes my stomach cramp, knowing I am concealing the truth about my forged identity I have lived under as Anna Čapková. I take my time to be sure I get my signature right—Ann Chapman—a name that gets me back to the States and annihilates my Czech existence as Anna *Čapková with one stroke of the pen.*

Even though I have willed myself to forget this episode, yoga's X-ray machine recaptures it during deep relaxation. I surrender to the sadness the memory brings up. Week after week, an oppressive sadness claims me during deep relaxation, sometimes with a story attached to it, like the day we went to the American Embassy; other times it is an amorphous feeling of loss and grief.

Then one day, when settled in corpse pose, I am filled with a sweet, comforting tranquility. It's as if I'm released from captivity, my chest light and airy. The burning sensation under my eyelids is gone, and with it the sadness that weighed on my chest like a heavy boulder. Did that sadness disappear because of a magical happening, or did I submit to my body's natural wisdom to let those feelings be felt and acknowledged? In awe of yoga's ability to penetrate hard to reach regions of my internal world, I liken this experience to what an X-ray machine does when it infiltrates the body for a diagnosis.

During my yoga practices, I come to understand that the birthing breath, a close cousin to a deep yogic breath, parallels the Lamaze breathing technique for riding the waves of childbirth contractions. Lamaze breathing lessens the pain of delivery just like yogic breathing lessens emotional and physical pain. Both the yogic and Lamaze breathing signal a new beginning, and for me, the eventual birth of a new self. A yoga practice lets me feel the way an X-ray machine lets me see what is hidden from sight. By revealing what is hidden from my awareness, yoga transforms sorrow into calm and loss into new possibilities.

Hungry to understand how yoga works, I acquire a sizeable collection of books on yoga history and philosophy. I learn that by copying the behavior of animals, the ancient yogis discovered that the physical sensation of a stretch calms the activity of the mind. To prepare for their meditation, they relied on stretches and deep breaths to subdue the mind's intrusive presence. These stretches eventually evolved into yoga postures that became a medium of communication between the body and the mind. This information sparks my desire to find out if this is so for my classmates as well.

Rosemary is a tall, thin woman in her late fifties who speaks in a soft voice with long pauses between sentences. After I compliment her watercolor landscapes exhibited at the local gallery, she shares her story. "Those paintings are my escape. My personal life is nothing like those peaceful landscapes," she says, then stops to consider how much she is willing to reveal. Pulling her shoulders forward like a wounded bird, she continues. "Recently, my marriage broke up. My adult bipolar daughter lives with me. Antonio's class is my salvation. Without yoga, I would probably be in a therapist's office."

I query a bubbly dark-haired middle-aged woman who is exuberant about yoga and planning to become a yoga teacher; college students for whom yoga is a fun break from their studies; a woman in her forties going through a protracted divorce;

and a slender gray-haired woman in her sixties struggling with the recent loss of her husband. Incapable of defining exactly what it is I am seeking, I instinctively conclude that staying with yoga is what I need. I will come to understand why yoga became so important to me much, much later.

I add Antonio's Thursday evening class to my tight schedule. Even these twice-a-week classes are not enough to satisfy what has come to be so important to me: removal from the events of the day, being an astute observer of my shifting moods and attitudes, and feeling better equipped to control my reactions.

I cannot tear myself away from the photographs of Desikachar's peaceful face as he demonstrates the yoga postures in his book *The Heart of Yoga: Developing a Personal Practice*. I want to feel that same contentment and absorption, which I never quite reach when doing yoga in class. How do I, as Desikachar suggests, develop that personal home practice that will deepen my relationship to yoga? And when will I find the time to do it? Dreaming of having that home practice, I acquire a turquoise yoga mat, two new yoga outfits, blocks, and instructional books to teach me about the structure and purpose of each yoga posture. I make my own strap for leg lifts and an eye bag filled with flax and lavender for deep relaxation. I have no idea how I will develop that home practice, but the power of yoga to act as an X-ray machine that reveals me to myself and purges me of an ancient sadness convinces me it needs to happen.

15: Lifting the Curtain

"We're here!" I cry out as we drive onto a grass-covered drive-way of our Prince Edward Island vacation cottage. Ahead, a barn-red cottage looks like an old lady with its faded white trim, crooked shutters, and a sagging front porch. Chirping birds welcome us as we tour the slanted rooms and oddly shaped porches. The unruly pine branches pressing against the oversized window convert the kitchen into a dark forest. The faint smell of mushrooms growing under those trees completes the illusion. A creaky staircase leads to two bedrooms: one sunlit and cheerful, the other dark and tranquil. We choose the sunny one with a sloping floor that faces the bay and name the shady one the Forest Room because of its narrow deck with spongy floorboards and proximity to the prickly pine trees.

"Is this how you imagined the cottage?" Dennis asks as he looks for a level spot for his wine glass.

"Yes! The Forest Room is perfect for starting up my home practice," I say, already imagining myself in a posture flow in the coolness of its seclusion.

"Good. It's rundown and rustic, but it has a lot of character. It feels good to be here."

I lift my glass. "To the next stage of my yoga adventure and a wonderful vacation!"

"How about afternoons of reading on the porch for me and yoga in the secluded Forest Room for you? And mornings will be beach walks and hikes," Dennis proposes, clinking my glass. With each sip of wine, our dilapidated cottage feels more like a palace.

The next day, welcomed by a strong scent of pine, I enter the Forest Room with my yoga supplies: mat, blocks, strap, handbooks, and folders with xeroxed sequences. I arrange my books on the wobbly desk under the window and my turquoise mat in the center of the room facing the trees visible from the porch. With great care, I spread the xeroxed sheets with postures around my mat in the order I plan to execute them. I study every detail about how to position my arms and legs, and when to inhale and exhale. To limber up, I run through a fifteen-minute warm-up, making sure every muscle and joint gets a chance to participate.

And so, here the real practice begins—the sun salutation twelve-movement flow Antonio does right after the warm-ups. In large letters, I write *I* for "inhale" and *E* for "exhale" next to each of the twelve postures to correctly coordinate my movements with my breaths. I run through the twelve movements with my eyes glued to the xeroxed sheet, then stepping to the top of the mat, I visualize the posture sequence before I go into it.

I bring myself into mountain, the starting pose of the sun salutation. Focused on a bright green cluster of pine needles, I snap into action.

"*Inhale* arms overhead, *exhale* into a forward bend. *Inhale* into a lunge…" The sound of Antonio's voice echoes through me as I work my way through the posture flow. "Open your chest. Inhale as you go into cobra. Now exhale as you glide into down dog." As his voice fades into the background, my own takes over: "Lunge forward with your right leg in preparation for a forward bend." The postures flow in a continuous chain as if I'm gliding on ice. Once, twice, three times, I repeat the sun salutation until I lose count.

The models on the xeroxed sheet become my accomplices in this spirited dance. I feel the internal logic of the postures I failed to notice when doing them in Antonio's class. In this serene setting, my breathing slows, as does the distracting activity of my mind. I delight in getting to know the different personalities and characteristics of the postures: arms outstretched and chest open disperses dark thoughts; a lengthening in my spine sends a tingle of aliveness up my spinal column; a seated twist pulls me out of my lethargy; head below my heart clears my mind.

Smiling at the yellow chickadee perched on the pine tree, I imagine myself in its place when I move into my tree pose. As soon as my spine wobbles, I deepen my breath and steady my gaze. Stunned, I regain my balance. *That's it,* I say to myself, *the combination of breath, an uncluttered mind, and steady focus is the recipe for a strong tree.*

In the pacifying isolation of the Forest Room, and with only myself to rely on, I pay close attention to the moment a sensation arrives and departs when lengthening my spine or rotating my hip. Pleased with my progress, I let each posture open like the petals of a blooming rose. The more I let my body ease its way into the posture, the more aware I am of its unique qualities and what my reactions are to the posture. Do I get frustrated when I can't do the posture the way I want to? Does the posture make me feel good about myself? Does the posture energize me? Does it relax me? Does it discourage me?

Craving action and movement, I never understood the purpose of standing and doing nothing when in mountain pose. This time, fighting back my tendency to rush through it so I can get to the more interesting postures, I stop to think about why it is called "mountain." I recall the hike my husband and I did a few weeks ago up Giant in Keene Valley: to reach the summit, I had to stretch my legs, climb from rock to rock, climb over boulders and fallen tree trunks, cross streams, reach my arms to clasp tree trunks when jumping over boulders, slide through patches of mud, sweat my way up a steep incline, scratch myself on prickly branches, get bitten by mosquitoes, and feel the burning sensation of salty perspiration dripping into my eyes. What on earth sustained me through the climb to that far-off summit?

Aside from the beauty of wildflowers; ferns shining in the sun; bubbling brooks; and towering birches, maples, and evergreens one sees along the hike, nothing equals the breathtaking splendor of what the world below looks like from that summit. Dirt, sweat, scratches, and bug bites are forgotten in that first gasp of wonder at small little me standing close to the sky surrounded by towering mountain peaks, lakes, houses, and roads on the scale of a dollhouse and gliding birds leaving short-lived shadows over the rolling mountaintops. Firmly grounded, I have become part of the mountain's long history and foreseeable future.

What I feel when I reach the summit of a mountain is comparable to how it feels in a yoga mountain pose when my feet are anchored, spine lengthened, arms reaching toward the sky, and gaze unmoving. When still like an immovable mountain, I can recreate the sensation of being on a mountain's summit when I am fully focused on what I am experiencing. The mountain anchors me, when I let it, like no other posture. Would I have changed my attitude toward the mountain posture without these two weeks to cultivate a connection to yoga's deeper purpose?

Nimble and euphoric, I run along the water's edge. My body, supple from two weeks of consistent yoga practice, feels firm and alive. The incoming waves wash over my toes, sending a tingling aliveness throughout my body. "Look, I'm a warrior!" I call out, burrowing my feet into the sand and stretching my arms into a five-pointed star stance. My head is high, my spine is extended, and my breaths are in sync with the cyclical movements of the waves. Bursting with energy, I wrap my arms around Dennis's waist and call to the flying gulls, "I'm a yogini, a yogini!" rolling that word on my tongue as if it is a sweet candy.

"I never knew that's what I married," Dennis says, pulling me toward the water to get our feet wet.

Back in Plattsburgh, I make my way to our sunlit bedroom to put on a T-shirt and loose-fitting lounging pants. I usually go straight to my study with a cup of coffee, but not today. I spread my mat by the altar table my parents brought from China. On it, I place a handwoven runner, a Ming Dynasty vase, a candle in a glass holder, and my favorite rock with crevices and indentations that feel comforting in the palm of my hand. Here, I intend to recreate the feel of the Forest Room where I practiced without Antonio's guidance to the invigorating scent of pine trees and tweeting birds.

I begin with centering in a cross-legged easy pose. Without blinking, I gaze at the wavering candle wick until my eyelids get heavy. Behind my closed eyes, I watch the floating image of the golden flame as it gets smaller and smaller. Composed and focused, I slide off my blue cushion, smile at the pink flower in my miniature vase, and blow out the candle. Once I am on my yoga mat, I go into a series of cat and dog spinal movements to prepare for the posture sequence I memorized on Prince Edward Island.

Guided by my inner teacher's voice, I gaze at the regal pine tree in my backyard, then light as a ballerina, I glide from down dog to cobra to pigeon, letting the power of the postures resonate. I melt into the relaxation pose as mind surrenders to body and body leads the mind. A voice in me repeats, first softly, then louder and louder: *You did it. You did it. You did it.* And I did.

16: *Showing Up*

"Ann, you should become an actress when you grow up," my mother used to say when I was small. "You would get to act out your emotions on stage instead of at home." It seems my mother was right. Now, a yoga practice is my stage for acting out a wide range of feelings and roles: happiness, distractibility, worry, sadness, anxiety, anger, determination, frustration, and empowerment. Some days, I find a soothing calm by burning off feelings of exhaustion and anxiety; other times, I leave the yoga mat ready to conquer the world. Each practice is governed by the narrative formulated by my body's response to the postures as they unveil the day's events and moods. I miss out on knowing that day's script if I do not show up on my yoga mat.

Usually disciplined about attending Antonio's evening class, one night my resolve wavers. Consumed by worry about Laura's upcoming breast cancer surgery on the other side of the Atlantic, teaching was tough going. Distracted and unfocused, I felt that time dragged. And then on top of that, a freshman from my composition class stopped by my office to bargain for a grade change. By the time he left, I wanted to curl up by our fireplace with a good book. But yoga? Where will I find the energy to make it through a ninety-minute class after a day like this?

When I reach the edge of the parking lot, I deliberate—should I turn right to go home or left toward the fitness center? My body tells me to turn left because yoga is what I need. I follow its directive like a mindless puppet.

The drama begins when I show up on my yoga mat.

Exhausted, hungry, anxious, and chilled to the bone, I lower my stiff body on the mat. The hardwood floor feels uncomfortable under my shoulder blades and hips. The fluorescent lights hurt my eyes. My legs and arms feel heavy, lifeless. A few deep breaths release some of the tension in my tight shoulders and spine, but my mind is an annoying jumble. To get away from my mind's activity, I visualize myself at the ocean's edge with sprays of salt water caressing my cheeks and gulls flying above the crashing waves. Just as I am about to immerse my toes in the water, Antonio's voice draws me into the present.

My body heavy and unresponsive, I roll to the side to push myself up. My movements sluggish, my head carrying on its intrusive drama, I let myself be lured by Antonio's gentle voice.

"Come into mountain for the sun salutation."

My Pavlovian responses override my angst, shaking me out of my stupor. On an inhale, I lengthen my spine and stretch my arms overhead. Leaning forward shuts off the mental chatter as if I am waving off a buzzing mosquito. My focus sharpens in down dog, and a barely noticeable smile forms in the corners of my mouth by the time I return to starting position. I anchor my legs and lift my arms while I discard, select, refurbish, and recycle the day's events. By the third round of sun salutations, I am alert and recharged. The sun salutation flow of twelve movements is my car wash. What drives out no longer resembles what drove in.

Antonio guides us into the bridge posture. Lying on my spine, knees bent and hips off the floor, soles of my feet and elbows pressing into the mat, I feel my legs shake, arms wobble, and hips droop. My frenetic breathing explodes like an overheated steam engine. *This is it. I can't hold this another second! I can't do it!* Certain my bridge is about to collapse, I latch onto the only tool left, my breath. Keeping my eyes fastened to a spot on the ceiling the way I did when using Lamaze breathing in childbirth, I breathe the panic out of my system. This strengthens my resolve to stay in the bridge. I repeat, "You can do this! Stay with it," and like the blue engine in *The Little Engine That Could*, I change *I think I can* to *I can*.

Antonio's voice comes back like a distant foghorn. "Start lowering your hips toward the mat vertebrae by vertebrae." This time, with legs and arms alive, spine and shoulders soft, mind removed from the concerns of the day, my spirits lift. Ever so slowly, I land on my mat elated to have defied my mind's negative presence and to discover I am capable of far more than I expected.

Our practice continues. I am on my belly, legs close to each other, hands under my shoulders in cobra. I lift my head, neck, and shoulders a tiny bit higher, but instantly my body rebels. My arms shaking, I am desperate to let go, but my pride won't let me. Noticing my struggle, Antonio leans over and whispers in my ear, "Ann, you're forcing too hard. Don't extend your spine so much."

I realize I must adjust the positioning of my hands to lessen the pressure on my spine. *Wow, it works!* Like a graceful swan with my neck and upper spine reaching toward the sky, I luxuriate in the feel of an elegant elongation of my upper body and a non-combative mind. Instead of struggling, I blend with the posture's natural purpose to strengthen and lengthen my spine, release tightness in the hips, and feel at home with myself. Instead of defeat, I feel a joyful victory.

As soon as I hear Antonio say tree posture, my mind goes wild. *Oh, no. Not today. I'm going to fall out of it. Please leave tree out of today's practice.* But I comply by placing my left foot against the inner thigh of my right leg. Before I have a chance to stabilize, my spine wobbles. Disappointed, my left foot slides down my leg, toes plunging toward the floor. *Why didn't I fall out of tree when I did it at home? What if I imagine the tree in my backyard is in front of me?* Again, I place my left foot against the inner thigh of my right leg. Breathing in and breathing out, I visualize the power of that pine tree growing inside me. I steady my body, letting my measured breathing take charge. Head high, standing foot firmly anchored on the floor, I open to the beauty of a stately tree with a mind as clear as a cloudless sky.

Each time I show up on the yoga mat, I confront my unadorned self. How does it feel when I push into a stretch with too much force, reach too far, fight my way into the posture instead of ease into it? Am I hunching my shoulders? Can I lengthen a bit more without straining? Is my jaw tight? My breathing too rapid? Can I get rid of my fear of falling out of the posture? Am I exploring my potential without prejudging what my edge should be? The postures are my working laboratory, the alphabet of my emotional self I get to act out each time I show up on my yoga stage.

One blustery winter day, classes are cancelled because of a fierce blizzard sweeping through Plattsburgh with unexpected force. Wild winds are making it difficult to get through the thickening snow. Picking up one boot out of the snow takes effort, only to be matched by the effort of picking up the other boot as the snow pulls it toward the ground. Snowflakes the size of corn flakes sting my cheeks and stick to my hat and coat. Frozen and wet, my cheeks burning and fingers purple and stiff, I finally reach my front door. My frozen fingers make it hard to get the key into the lock.

A hot bath warms me up but does not dissolve my heartache. Laura's voice sounded weak the other day when she called from the hospital after her mastectomy. "More treatments, more waiting, more worry and anxiety, more lifestyle adjustments," she wept into the phone over a thousand miles away. *How will Laura get through this without me? How will I manage being separated from her?* Crestfallen, I begrudge my teaching obligations for preventing me from being with her.

I decide to do the yoga practice on an exercise video I checked out of the library. I roll my mat out near the living room glass doors, keeping my eyes on the outdoor drama that simulates my own. A beautifully proportioned blond in a tight-fitting purple outfit who's smiling from ear to ear appears on the screen. She starts the practice with a cycle of deep yogic breaths. My chest is tight, my breaths short and rapid. My mind is with Laura in Cambridge, England.

My movements are mechanical. An image of Laura's body tensed with pain, her face pale and eyes sad, distracts me from the instructor's narrative. Unable to concentrate, I consider quitting, something I never do. The instructor's smiling voice overrides my intention when I hear her say, "Separate your legs four feet apart for warrior II."

Obediently, I move into a wide lunge.

"Feel the energy radiate from the center of your body," she chirps enthusiastically. I lift my shoulders and open my chest. I release a deep sigh. My drooping head straightens. Energy trickles back into my limp legs. Focused on the sensations that are energizing my body, I know what I need to do.

I run up to my study to dial Laura's number. "Laura, I'll be in Cambridge by Friday. We will get through this together. We can't let the Atlantic Ocean keep us apart," I say in a voice cracking with emotion.

"Oh, Ann, knowing you'll be here is already making me feel better."

I call a colleague to explain my predicament. I call my husband to get me a flight ticket. In three days, Laura and I tearfully fold into each other's arms.

It took a lot of cobras, trees, warriors, and sun salutations before I understood that a posture reflects my inner state the way a mirror reflects my image. Warrior II got me in touch with my true feelings, which got me to act on them. Profound change comes through the act of doing. The postures are the catalyst that spurs me into action. And for that to happen, I must show up on my yoga stage for that day's drama to be known and felt in every pore of my body as the movements transmit my ever-changing feelings and responses to my awaiting brain center.

17: Grandma Beckons

I am in down dog with my head suspended below my heart in Antonio's class. The deep stretch from the base of my heels to my hips and then back down toward my head sends an alarming shiver down my spine. A series of cyclical breaths pull me out of the present. As if the stage curtain to the past is lifted, my grandmother Ethel's face flashes in front of my eyes. Her lips are moving, but I can't decipher the words. The muscles in my legs and spine tighten, and my breathing goes haywire. And along with it explodes the pain and hurt I felt when I left her home as a young woman, never to return.

It is the summer of 1964, and I am a counselor at the Spring Valley Camp for the Blind, a short distance from my grandparents' home in Monsey, New York. A fellow counselor offers to drive me to their home in Monsey. My mother urges me to visit, and though not sure I am ready to face the pain of our enforced separation, I accept his offer.

My legs shaky, I walk toward a house on a pleasant tree-lined residential street that corresponds to the address in my hand. I tidy up my bouquet of drooping flowers and run my fingers through my ruffled hair, wiping the sweat off my forehead. My heart skips a beat when I see the name Shulman underneath the doorbell. I reach for the bell and then pull my hand away as if an electric shock hit me. I swallow a few times to moisten my dry throat and force my thumb on the bell. How do I introduce myself? *Hello, this is your lost granddaughter. I'm finally here.* But before I have a chance to decide what to say, the door opens, and there she is, a small-framed woman in a pale blue housedress, soft white hair pulled back in a bun, eyes curiously scanning my face.

"Ann?" Her voice is small to match her frame.

"That's me," I reply, my voice matching the timbre of hers. "Grandma Ethel, I…"

"Please come in. We're expecting you," she says, waving her hand toward a short white-haired man in a black suit and tight-fitting yarmulke. Examining their faces as if studying a museum painting, I recognize Belle's warm smile and lively eyes in my grandmother's face. I hoped for hugs or squeals of joy. I get an unnerving silence, punctuated by the unspoken awareness of the fourteen-year rift none of us talks about. The aroma of homemade food lets me know I have been expected, but the emotional distance says I'm not really wanted.

"Are these Uncle Avi's children?" I point to a row of framed photographs of dark-haired children with inquisitive eyes. It hurts to realize I have no right to expect Laura and I would be included with our displayed cousins.

"Yes, he has a large family," my grandmother explains. "Avi and his wife teach at the yeshiva." She stops in mid-thought as if it is all too complicated to bring me up to date on what I have missed out on.

Without encouraging me to help serve, she disappears in the kitchen. Seated at the head of the table, my grandfather waits in uncomfortable silence for her to return before starting a mealtime prayer. Fidgeting with my napkin, I lower my eyes while they pray in Hebrew, a language foreign to me. That familiar knot tightening my stomach returns. The steam rising from the soup tureen distracts me from the sound of their moving lips.

There are no questions about our family past, my sister, or my parents. They avert their eyes when I casually mention something about our life in Prague. What would they want to know about me? Anything at all? I refrain from mentioning Laura because my mother already cautioned me her marriage to a non-Jew places her permanently out of their lives. Where I fit into their lives is uncertain.

My grandmother explains how to make blintzes when I ask and encourages me to have more. I barely manage to eat what she already put on my plate. Did my free-spirited, radical-thinking mother really come from this devout household? After the meal, my grandfather retreats to his armchair in the neatly arranged, stuffy living room. Disregarding my presence, he buries his head in one of the Hebrew books he takes off the round table covered with a dainty white doily.

Dismissed. Unacknowledged. Unwanted.

"How about a walk?" my grandmother says when she returns from the kitchen. "Fresh air will do us both some good."

Along the way, my grandmother, like a Monsey celebrity, greets the people we pass. While she chats with a woman in a long dress and formal black hat in a mixture of Yiddish and English, I seem to have been forgotten.

"Will you be at the synagogue for tomorrow's performance?" the woman asks.

"Of course. Our grandchildren are in the play."

Feeling ignored, I shift impatiently from foot to foot waiting to be introduced. After resuming our interrupted walk, I ask in a hurt voice, "Why didn't you tell her I'm your granddaughter?"

"After you left, we were hounded by the FBI for information about where you were. We moved from Spring Valley to Monsey to start our lives as a family of three." She stops to catch her breath. "Nobody in Monsey knows we have a daughter, so how can I have a grown granddaughter?"

"Sooo, I don't exist?" My voice is barely audible. Her only response is a long sigh.

Later that evening, I shout into the phone when I call Belle to report about the visit. "Don't you ever, ever make me visit your parents again! I'm an alien in their home. Banished from their lives! Is this what vanishing like criminals did to our family relationships? I'm finished with them."

"Ann, I'm sorry it turned out this way. I appreciate you tried. From now on, I'll deal with my family on my own. I wish I could take you in my arms and squeeze that pain out of you. You do know how much I love you."

By the time I release the hold in down dog, the flashback from that visit has slipped back to my memory's archive, leaving me sad and depleted.

A full year after that brief but painful encounter with my grandmother, I have another vision. Practicing yoga in our bedroom, I am bathing in the perfumed spring air coming through our open glass doors. Luxuriating in a deep stretch, I let out a pleasurable sigh. Then, leaning into a standing forward bend, an image appears in my mind's eye: I see the smooth surface of a pond bathed in sunlight, with my grandmother Ethel on a bench with her hands in her lap. She motions for me to sit next to her. Her warm smile melts my heart. As she stretches her hand to caress my cheek, I cry out, "Grandma! I have so much to tell you."

Still folded forward with my fingertips on the floor and my belly resting on my thighs, I see her vanish as suddenly as she appeared. Was this a mirage? Or a message from my subconscious that something has changed? Where is the anger and hurt I felt when she made her first appearance a year ago?

When my practice is over, I gaze into the bright candlelight on my Chinese altar table, hoping to figure out why I feel so calm and content. What changed? In a single word: perspective.

Shifting my understanding to her perspective released compassion for the tragic predicament we both found ourselves in. This is what I would have told her if I had the chance: "You're as much a victim of my parents' actions as I was. I understand you never intended to reject me. You were rejecting Abe and

Belle's radical choices, which caused you and my grandfather so much pain."

And though this realization comes too late to repair the harm during my grandmother's lifetime, I realize it will make a big difference in how I live with that part of my past from now on. Would I have arrived at a change in perspective without yoga's prodding to confront the inner chaos I brought with me the day I joined Antonio's class?

18: Asserting My Voice

Nestled in snug armchairs in our favorite coffee shop, I have a need to unburden myself. "I'm in limbo, Margo. I find my mind wandering during Antonio's class. After two and a half years, I can do his routine with closed eyes. I need something more, but I don't know what."

Ever perceptive, Margo smiles wider. "Tell me more."

My eyes look up to the ceiling, my habit in thinking through an issue. "Plateau, I think."

"Mmm," she says. "It happens to most of us. After a while, we learn as much as there is in one setting and we need to move on."

"You mean, actually leave the class? If not for him, I doubt I would have stayed with yoga. I feel so indebted to him."

"There are other teachers, and each one has a personal style. Your restlessness is a sign you need to be introduced to a different approach."

My eyes have reached that spot on the ceiling again. "Okay, I need more of a bounce, a challenge to move forward. Ugh, though, I don't want to hurt his feelings. I hate being in this bind…"

"Are you ready for a *dramatic* change?" she asks, enticing me with a grin and a meaningful silence. "Carmen!" Margo exclaims. "She's on Main Street. I've heard she can barely fit her devotees into her studio."

"Honestly, I don't know if I can do this to Antonio. He has brought me from nowhere to here. Where would I be without him?" Waiting for Margo to stir the foam on her cappuccino, I shift back and forth in my seat, hoping for a solution.

"Ann," she says, placing her cup on the table, "we all get stale and need other experiences to stretch. It's important to graduate from one level to the next. I'm certain you're not the first student who has left his class."

"It feels like betrayal."

My memory flashes to how reticent I was at age fifteen to voice my objection after Abe's announcement that we were moving to China. *Am I following the same pattern in this comparatively minor situation?*

Margo's voice brings me back to our unfinished conversation. "What have you got to lose? If you're not challenged in Carmen's class, Antonio will always be glad to have you back. These decisions are rarely fatal." That wide grin again. "You're making assumptions about Antonio without knowing how he will react. Why not be honest and let *him* tell you how *he* feels about it. Don't forget this is about you, not Antonio. I'm sure he will see it that way."

Squeezing Margo's hand, I add, "Your way of sticking to the point is helpful."

Though Abe and Belle are no longer alive, their ghost-like presence still challenges my self-sufficiency. But I decide this will be a good chance to practice a new strategy and to take a stand on something that matters to me. In warrior II, I say to others and myself, "This is who I am; this is how I take charge of my life." So why can't I do it off the yoga mat?

A few days later, I stand back and wait while the students straggle out of the aerobics room before I approach Antonio. My eyes lowered toward the floor, I clear my throat one last time. "Antonio, I, I, I've been thinking about expanding my practice." I lift my eyes to see the effect of my words. "Perhaps even try a different style of yoga." My breath is slowing as he waits for me to finish. "I'm deeply grateful for all I've learned from you."

Worried he will disapprove, I jump to the point. "But it's time for a change." My voice stronger, I add, "I'm thinking of taking Carmen's class." Studying his face for a clue about his feelings, I fill in the silence. "But leaving your class is hard for me." Flushed and out of breath, I look up at his calm, kind face with trepidation.

"Carmen was once my student. You'll be in good hands. I also studied with a variety of teachers in my early yoga days. It's a sign you're ready to move forward," he says, easing my discomfort.

"You taught me everything I know. Your love of yoga had a huge effect on me. I can never thank you enough for what you've given me." Under his approving look, the tension in my shoulders dissipates like air out of a balloon.

"It was great watching you blossom into a yogini. I wish you the very best. Stop by to let me know how things are going. And give my regards to Carmen."

He puts the palms of his hands together and bows his head with the Sanskrit greeting *namaste* (I bow to you) and a warm smile of consent. Deeply touched, my chest heaves as I move toward the door.

Then, like a blast of hot air, the full impact of my severance hits me. *Why on earth am I doing this? Do I really need to venture into the untried? Wouldn't I be better off staying with Antonio?* Ambivalence kicks in. Then again, I reason, *Antonio was supportive. Gotta snap out of this, Ann, it is time to trust your inner voice. Besides, Antonio made it clear that without change there is no growth. It's time for a new adventure.*

Carmen's studio has an inviting waiting room decorated in soft beige. A slender woman in her early fifties with beautiful long, wavy chestnut hair and vivacious eyes greets each of us with a nod of her head and a warm smile. Her studio has a homey feel in comparison to the aerobics room in the college fitness center. The contemporary art and a desk with books and plants in the far corner of the studio subdue some of my nervousness. A middle-aged woman in a chartreuse yoga outfit moves her mat to make room for me. "Welcome to the class," she says in a pleasant voice, "you'll love it." Grateful for the encouragement, I place my mat next to hers and introduce myself.

Class starts. Hawklike, I follow every move of Carmen's pliable body, afraid I will miss something important. I can't help comparing her style to Antonio's, who guides us through a fixed routine with verbal cues, rarely doing the postures with us the way Carmen does. I trust she will reveal the posture's mystery with her well-chosen words and mindful movements. I replicate her every gesture as closely as I can. Periodically, Carmen steps off her mat to correct our misalignments. With a self-assured touch of her hand, she guides my hip or shoulder to where each should be until I feel the posture's correct composition.

My eyes fill with tears when Carmen adjusts my head in corpse pose near the end of the class with her soft hands. I feel I have been lovingly tucked into bed, safe and coddled. In response to her touch, my muscles melt like warm wax. Carmen ends the class with the poem "Allow" by Danna Faulds from *Go In and In: Poems from the Heart of Yoga*. The last lines of the poem confirm Antonio's advice to look at change as a step forward:

> "In the choice to let go of your
> known way of being, the whole
> world is revealed to your new eyes."

When class is over, my yoga neighbor asks, "Was I right?"
"Can't wait for next week," I say in a dreamlike voice.

One wintry evening, a wild snowstorm that closes local schools and makes driving a hazard keeps most of the students home. Carmen's fluid movements create a meditative mood. Her soothing voice is hypnotic, calming. Preparing to place my right foot against my left upper thigh, I am drawn to the beauty of the steady flow of fluffy snowflakes lighting up the surrounding darkness. Transfixed, I forget about my fear of falling out of my tree. Of its own accord, it grows into a powerful northern pine, reaching up and up as what I see outside and feel within merge into harmony.

Driving home through the snow-covered streets, I still feel the reverberations from the tree I did in Carmen's class. What makes it so memorable? I think of what I learned back in the Polish village Bortne in the Carpathian Mountains, when Dennis's cousin Nikolaj milked his cows. The sun was setting when he moved his four cows into the barn. I followed him to see how he milks the cows. Surprised why he didn't start milking them right away, I asked what he was waiting for.

"The cows can't be rushed," he told me. "They just got into the barn, and they need to adjust. Their milk will not be as good if I milk them immediately. I have to take it slowly."

I immediately see the connection to a centering we do before a yoga practice. Slowing down before I go into my practice gives me a deeper practice. For the cows, slowing down gives them time to produce their best milk. If only I could take life like a cow!

Yoga is teaching me that to create my best postures, my alignment, range of motion, breath, and mindset need to be in balance. Nikolaj taught me an important lesson about how symmetry and balance work in the world of nature. I need to transpose that knowledge to the way I practice yoga. Now I understand how that symmetry feels emotionally and spiritually the moment my body and mind converge in a natural and easeful oneness. I, like the cows, produce my best when centered and in balance with myself.

Grateful to Margo and Antonio for their support, I no longer doubt I made the right decision to advance my yoga journey by asserting my voice at the right time and in the right way. It takes more than showing up on my yoga mat for exhilarating things to happen; it takes setting the course of action in the right direction.

19: A Tempting Proposal

I have been silent for a long time, but suddenly I feel an urge to hold a pen to mediate between my mind and heart. I am more than what transpires during the day—the classes I teach, the domestic chores I do, my interactions, the miles I walk, or the yoga postures I hold. Finding myself on the threshold of a new beginning, I am ready to enter the unknown and untried. How better to give these feelings expression and meaning than to write about them in my journal?

Although the physical results of my daily practices are noticeable in my improved strength, stamina, and balance, other important, less visible things are happening. Resuming my journal writing after two years of self-imposed silence is a sign that my yoga practice is melting the protective shield around my heart. I feel like Sleeping Beauty, who was awakened from her hundred-year sleep by the prince's kiss. The prince, whose kiss will awaken me to a new dawn, arrives at a cocktail party in a yoga disguise.

My friend Claire, a vivacious bright-eyed woman my age, calls me over to meet her friend Lilian, who just completed her teacher training at the Kripalu Yoga Center in Lenox,

Massachusetts. "I already told her about your passion for yoga," she explains as she introduces us.

"How long have you been doing yoga?" I ask when we move to a quiet part of the room.

"I fell in love with yoga in my fifties. And now, I'm teaching my first yoga class in the lobby of the National Bank in downtown Plattsburgh. Stop by if you're interested."

My curiosity building, I ask, "What was the training like? What yoga books did you study for your certification? What's it like teaching yoga?"

"The Kripalu staff is first-rate. The training is tough but the best thing I ever did. And though the first class I taught was a bit shaky, I quickly adjusted. The students are so appreciative! But I seem to have struck a chord with you. Have you thought about teaching yoga?"

"Teach yoga? Never crossed my mind. Not in my wildest dreams," I say, feeling my face turn red and my certainty shaken. "Frankly, I don't think I have a brain for that. I'm strictly a humanities person, though I really love yoga. I'm comfortable teaching a novel to forty students, but explaining how to get in and out of a posture would put me over the edge."

Lilian smiles understandingly. "If you decide to go to Kripalu, let me know. You can borrow the books I used in preparation for the training," she adds casually as we join the others at the buffet.

My mind is whirling like a roller coaster. I know I am skilled at teaching novels, poetry, ideas, and languages, but none of these subjects brings me out of my head and into my body. *Teaching yoga is a thoroughly absurd proposition,* I tell myself. *Besides, at fifty-nine, I'm too old to even think of doing such a crazy thing. But then again, Lilian is about my age, and she did it. Well, that's Lilian, not me.* Despite my efforts to stop thinking about it, the idea of teaching yoga persists.

The following evening, Dennis is chopping vegetables when I walk into the kitchen and start blurting: "Ever since Lilian planted the idea of teaching yoga in my head, I've been in a quandary. The whole thing is nuts, but…at the same time, I'm excited to raise the level of my yoga practice and to share my love of yoga with others. Can you make sense of this?"

He replaces the sharp end of the knife into the butcher block. He pauses. Then what he says shocks me. "I've noticed a lot of positive changes in you since you've begun your practice."

"Are the changes that visible?" I know exciting things have been happening in me, but I thought they were private, internal.

"Your attitude toward life is more wondrous, and you take things more slowly. You're more confident, calmer, and most importantly, happier. Take time to think it through, but really, you're a born teacher, so why not try teaching yoga?"

I realize I've made my decision. "Okay, you've convinced me. No need to waste any more time. I'm off to find the phone number for Kripalu."

"How can I help you?" a young man with a pleasant voice asks when I make the call.

"First, I should tell you I'm almost sixty." My heart sinking, I continue in a hushed voice. "Am I too old to become a yoga teacher?"

"Not at all. Age is not an impediment. It can even be an advantage. Our older students make wonderful teachers because they bring so much life experience to their teaching."

I swallow hard before I continue. "In that case, let's hit my list of questions."

I pour my love for yoga into my application essay, reassured that my thirty years of teaching, accrued life experiences, and time spent raising a family are as important as flexibility and youth. My yoga future hangs in suspense the moment I drop my letter in the mailbox.

Two months later, I am getting ready for the first of three nine-day sessions of yoga teacher training. My mind is swirling with questions. Will everybody in the program be young and slim? Will I be the oldest and least fit? Will I be able to memorize the new material? Will I have the stamina to keep up with the yoga practices? Will I pass the tests? Will I be comfortable in a large dorm room? Am I meant to be a yoga teacher? Will I survive on a vegetarian diet, and God forbid, no coffee? Through this cacophony, I pack my bag.

Kripalu, here I come!

Part III:

Shiva's Dance of Destruction and Creation

"It is true, we do share some memory in the brain, but by far, the deeper, older messages are stored in the body and must be accessed through the body. Your body is your subconscious mind, and you can't heal it by talk alone."

—Candace B. Pert
Molecules of Emotion:
The Science Behind Mind Body Medicine

20: *Metamorphosis, Stage One*

It is a cold January morning in 2002 when my son Daniel, who's
visiting over the Christmas holiday, and I pull out of the drive-
way and head for Lenox, Massachusetts, where I'll begin my
yoga teacher training at Kripalu. The drive is four and a half
hours, and each mile brings me closer to my desired goal: to
deepen my knowledge of yoga and to get certified to teach. The
moment we reach the Berkshire mountains, fluffy snowflakes
drape the trees and mountains in white robes. Straining to see
through their film on the car window, I am the first one to spot
a sign for Kripalu. We pass Tanglewood with regal mountain
peaks in the distance and arrive at a modest stone gate with a
small light-blue sign, the word *Kripalu* scrolled in white letters.

Abiding by the reduced speed limit, Daniel slows to a crawl.
We drive past towering evergreens with branches weighted
down with fresh snow before we see the outline of a large brick
building.

"What's awaiting me behind those glass doors?" I say in a
timid voice.

"I'm sure it will all work out," Daniel says like a loving par-
ent sending a child off to camp.

The vast windows of the lobby face the glimmering mountains on the other side of Lake Mahkeenac. An urn of herbal tea and a bowl of fresh fruit are there to welcome the new arrivals. At the registration desk, I receive my program schedule, room assignment, and a YTT tag that I pin to my shirt so I blend in with the rest of the Kripalu residents. Yogis (male practitioners of yoga) and yoginis (female practitioners of yoga) walking through the hallways in stylish yoga outfits with mats under their arms convey a sense of purpose and enthusiasm. The class offerings posted on large bulletin boards leave me dazed: Ayurvedic balance in the body systems, meditation practices, drumming, chanting, yoga-dance classes, and workshops with titles like "Heal Yourself, Heal Your Life" and "Unlock Your Body's Story." Not accustomed to associating me with these kind of activities, Daniel lifts his eyebrows. I shrug and smile apprehensively.

Testimonies about the healing impact of Kripalu teachings on the walls of the busy hallways deliver moving stories of personal transformation: from inner chaos to a balanced calm, from a poor self-image to a sense of wholeness, from destructive tendencies to a healthier lifestyle.

I peek into a large dining room with long tables, the carpeted main chapel, and spacious practice rooms: Sunrise, Sunset, Mountain, and Forest. Four flights of stairs take me from the whirlpool in the basement to the Silent Room, where residents sip tea, read, and write in their journals in armchairs that face the mountain view. Past the Healing Arts massage rooms, I take the staircase to the Kripalu shop with books on yoga philosophy, spirituality, anatomy, yoga postures, and meditation. The subtle aroma of candles and incense permeates its selection of yoga clothing, mats, meditation cushions, essential oils, gemstones, and CDs with music for yoga practices and meditation. *Antonio would be right at home here!* I smile at the thought of him in this setting.

A black-and-white photograph of the bald Swami Kripalu presides over it all, his black eyes radiating a deep inner strength and compassion. A swami is a yogi initiated into a religious monastic order. *I bet this man has something important to teach me,* I think, *but who exactly is he? And why is this place named after him?*

Back in the lobby, I approach a young woman with bouncy ponytails and cute dimples welcoming newcomers. "Could you please tell me who Swami Kripalu is?" I ask.

"Kri-pah-*loo*," she responds pleasantly, emphasizing the last syllable. "In Hindi, it means *compassion.* Kripalu yoga is based on Swami Kripalu's teachings on love, practice, and self-development."

I deposit this information in my memory bank for future exploration.

First to arrive in the bright dorm room, I put my things on a low bunk bed under a window facing the mountains. As I'm unzipping my suitcase, the door flings open, hitting the side wall. I jump at the thud.

"Sorry!" A huge grin flashes, disarming me. A woman leans over to pick up the dropped bulging suitcase and a yoga mat, all while balancing an oversized bag draped over her shoulder.

"I'm Joy," she announces as she plops all her bags, coat, and gloves on one of the beds, then moves the pile to flop down on her back.

"Hi, I'm Ann."

"I'm so glad to be here after a fourteen-hour drive from Ohio! I'm beat. But! No time to dally! Is this your first time?" she asks, changing focus.

"Yes. And you?"

Her lively brown eyes sparkle. "I'm an old-timer. Kripalu is my lifeline." Jumping up, she reaches into her suitcase and pulls out an orange yoga outfit, which she tosses on the bed. Undressing, she explains, "We have to hurry. Stephen Cope is teaching this afternoon's 4:30 p.m. yoga practice." She emphasizes the name with a look of respect buttressed by excitement.

Infected by her enthusiasm, I slip into an oversized T-shirt and baggy pants, grab my turquoise mat, and follow her through the maze of hallways and doorways. "This," Joy whispers, pointing to a packed room, "is the Forest Room." I make a mental note to find out why this is an important place.

A middle-aged man in a navy-blue yoga outfit is warming up with graceful slow movements on an elevated carpeted platform in the front of the room. A few people push their mats over to make room for us. My eyes remain riveted on what Steve Cope is doing. He soon addresses the class in a soft, soothing voice.

The hour-and-a-half class passes with time-travel speed. I feel a connection between the spirit of Cope's practice and the expression in Swami Kripalu's eyes telling me to *slow down, be present, be yourself*. Tall trees visible from the windows remind me of *my* Forest Room on Prince Edward Island where I worked on decoding yoga's system of postures. My reverie is broken when Joy says, "We better get to the dining room if we're going to make it to class on time."

We speed-walk to the cafeteria, where the vegetarian dishes look especially inviting. I ask Joy, "Is it as tasty as it looks?"

"I'm a vegetarian. Their cookbook is my bible," she says, filling her plate with raw vegetables and a tofu stir-fry. Copying her, I load up. We quicken our pace to grab the two empty seats in the back of the room.

"So, you're in YTT?" the woman next to me asks after she examines my tag. "My husband and I are in a relationship workshop." She nods toward the man sitting across from her who looks unsure about tasting the clump of tempeh dangling on his fork.

Raising my eyebrows, I point to a young man, deep in thought, with a bright yellow tag that says "Silence" in big letters. Joy immediately understands. "He's in a silent retreat. He won't speak until his retreat is over in a few days."

Not the quiet type, I whisper, "Is that for real? Why would anyone want to go on a silent retreat?"

"You sure are a novice! Stick with me," she laughs. "I'll make you one of us in no time. I think you'll be a perfect fit for this place once you get to know how things work here. Look, it's time for class." She taps me on the shoulder to pick up my tray and head toward the drop-off bins.

"And this," she says with dramatic flair after we descend the staircase to the ground floor, "is the Shadowbrook Room where we'll have our training."

The room is large enough to accommodate a hundred people. It has a thick wall-to-wall beige carpet, long rows of windows on both sides of the room, and a podium in the front of the room. In the back of the room, there are closets with yoga equipment, stacked BackJack chairs (ergonomic chairs with back support for sitting on the floor), and bulletin boards for announcements and attendance sheets with our names. I am intrigued by the bronze statue of a man encased in a circle with four arms playing on a drum and dancing over flames. He is positioned in the center of the podium next to a life-sized skeleton.

"What's the story behind that smiling statue?"

"That's Lord Shiva in a cosmic dance of destruction and creation. Though it's more complicated than that, it has something to do with the transformational process."

"Hmm, my life has put me through cycles of change and loss I would hardly call a joyful dance—more like a confrontation on a battlefield," I say semiseriously. "Maybe I have something to learn from Lord Shiva about the relationship between what is being destroyed and what is being created in its place."

"I can see there's a reason you're so interested in him."

"I hope to find that out before I leave this place."

By now all sixty students, two instructors, and four assistants are seated on black BackJacks in a large circle. The collective anticipation of this new common adventure electrifies the air. With a microphone in hand, a man in his forties with penetrating eyes that remind me of Swami Kripalu's addresses the class. "My name is Yoganand. Martha and I," he says, turning to the kind-looking, attractive woman next to him, "will be your instructors for the duration of your training. Tomorrow, we start formal instruction. Tonight, we'll get to know each other a bit." With a cheerful spark in his eyes, he passes the mike to Martha.

"Welcome to YTT," she says. "Please give a *brief* introduction describing where you're from and why you're here." With a motherly smile, she passes the mike to a young woman with a bushy head of hair dressed in a stunning yoga outfit.

My body stiffens, and my mind goes into a wild spin. *What can I say about my yoga accomplishments? These people all look like they belong here. I feel like an imposter.* By the time the mike is thrust at me, my hands are sweaty and my face is bright red. The sound in the back of my throat expels, gravelly and slow: "I'm Ann...from Plattsburgh, New York...to...to...learn more about yoga. I've been practicing yoga for the past two and a half years." Squeezing my voice through my tightened chest, I conclude, "I love yoga." That's it. I drop the mike in the lap of the person next to me, lower my eyes, and avoid others' stares. Finally, and importantly, my big reveal is over. I am still here. My blood pressure has lowered, the mike is passed, the group has moved on.

"Please stack the BackJacks in the back of the room," Martha says while Yoganand puts on lively Latin dance music.

"Make up your own steps. Have fun," he encourages.

Making her way to the center of the room, a young woman swirls her long hair and sways her body gracefully. *Okay, I say to myself, I'm a good dancer—I can do this.* Except my body feels rigid, and as hard as I try, I can't mimic the young woman's expressive style. I teeter as I execute my shuffle. Self-conscious and convinced that everyone is looking at me, I begin again. Determined now, mind over matter, my feet move to the seductive rhythms. *Good try, Ann!* It's still a flimsy attempt. Then, true to form, a voice in my head says, *Don't try so hard. Relax.*

Beginning anew, I pick my right foot up then put it down, only slightly unstable. Trying to balance, I plant both feet side by side. Still stuck in molasses, I almost tip over. I assume everyone is watching, but when I pick my head up, I see they are all into their own thing. When I let the music lead me, my feet begin to cooperate. Soon I am the light-footed, spontaneous Ann of old. *Be yourself,* says my inner voice, *don't let your head rule.*

A smiling assistant hands me a piece of pink paper in the shape of a diamond to write down my intention for this session. Effortlessly, I write in large letters: *Inner integrity. Personal direction.* I join the other students to hang my intentions on the wall behind Lord Shiva. *So, is this my personal quest? Integrity and direction? Not a bad beginning.* I wink at dancing Shiva, who might know better than I do where my quest is taking me.

At 5:00 a.m., the alarm goes off for the daily spiritual practice to nurture the mind and body called a sadhana. Sleepy dorm mates and I make our way to the Shadowbrook Room. My measure of success will be if the instructor is an Antonio or a Carmen. Gentle flute music brushes away the last traces of sleepiness. Lit candles nestled in Shiva's four hands shed light on his gleeful face. I place my mat in front of the skeleton so I can identify the parts of my body I am using in the postures. Shiva's transformational dance is happening all around me: the darkness of night transitioning into daylight, sluggishness into aliveness, stiffness into fluidity, and stillness into movement.

Our young instructor's suave movements seem to materialize from the depths of her being. I synchronize mine with hers. The beauty of the postures is being transferred to me through the fluid movements of her athletic body. Beads of sweat on her upper lip and under her armpits make me wonder if I am working as hard as she is. As if I'm gliding across a polished dance floor, my movements send a pleasant tingle from my arms to the ball mounts of my toes. I am expressing through postural forms what a ballerina does through pliés, allegros, and allonges when dancing to magical music in the chorus line in *Swan Lake*.

When the instructor prompts us to identify what we are feeling, I am astonished at the thrilling surge of energy pulsing under the surface of my skin and sending a warm glow throughout my body. Gone are my hunger pangs, joint and muscle crankiness, and awareness of others. I am captive to the subtle movements of my energized body. When wrapped in a soft blue blanket, I melt into deep relaxation, muscles pliant and organs massaged. I silently hum Beethoven's "Ode to Joy."

Balancing a tray with miso soup, a freshly baked pecan scone, a bowl of fresh fruit, and a glass of milk, I find a spot near a window with a pastoral view of a tree-covered slope sparkling in the white snow. The silent breakfast, a Kripalu tradition, allows me to hear my own thoughts. I watch a young woman absorbed in journal-writing and a woman my age holding her hands above her cereal bowl in silent prayer. She looks blissful. *I'd like to try something like that if it doesn't make me self-conscious. It would be fun to make up my own prayer.* Without the distraction of conversation, the flavors and textures of my food are more intense than usual. On my way out of the dining room, I admit how special it is to be in my own company.

In our first class, we receive the 300-page *Kripalu Yoga Teacher Development* manual. *How will I ever get through all of this?* I wonder. Yoganand welcomes us to, as he says, the study of "the true spirit of the ancient art and science of yoga" by quoting Swami Kripalu. "Yoga is the meeting of the drop with the ocean. The ultimate result of all yoga is purity of mind and body." I love the image of little me merging with the larger universe.

The definition of yoga's aim addresses my emotional needs directly when I read it in the manual. "The ability to know all parts of our selves with compassionate self-awareness, and to maintain contact with our core Self in the face of all difficulty and disturbing events of our passing lives becomes the balm that quiets the colliding thoughts, eases hurt in the body, and assuages the desperate emotions." *So is this why my relationship with the postures has had such a profound effect on me?*

The table of contents states the goals for this training: understanding and mastering yoga philosophy, the Kripalu yoga teaching methodology, warm-ups and twenty-six yoga postures, basic pranayama (breathing) techniques, meditation, lesson planning, and anatomy and physiology. The opening lecture begins, once again, with the words of Swami Kripalu. "How can speech have access to those places where the mind cannot go? Speech can describe sensory experiences but not extrasensory ones." *So this is all about what happens on a nonverbal level! Am I ready to find out what that means for me?*

The morning zips by between lectures and hands-on exercises and posture practices that teach the art of letting go by releasing energy blocks. Yoga turns out to be a subject of study full of fascinating revelations and discoveries. There is so much I want to know, so much I want to understand, and so much I had never thought about. My head is spinning from all the new theories and tactile experiences. I welcome the time-out for lunch to clear my head.

Afterward, Joy approaches me. "How about that promised tour of the Kripalu grounds? I'm dying for fresh air!"

So am I, and snuggled into our winter clothing, we make our way to frozen Lake Makhoenac, admiring along the way the rows of fir trees that date back to the nineteenth century.

"When did you start doing yoga?" I ask Joy.

"I first saw it on TV. Our small town had no yoga teachers. I bought books, tapes, and DVDs to learn it on my own. I also attended retreats and workshops with renowned yogis. Then

I discovered Kripalu. After this training, I'll be the first yoga teacher in Columbus, Ohio!"

"Wow, what determination!"

"Aren't you here because you love yoga?"

"I certainly am," I say, adjusting my stride to match hers. My concerns about our twenty-year age difference quickly dissolve. "What do you know about the history of Kripalu? I've never experienced a place like this."

"Kripalu started in the 1970s when Amrit Desai founded a monastic yoga center in Somneytown, Pennsylvania. He named it Kripalu Healing Arts to honor his guru Swami Kripalu."

"How did they end up here?"

"In 1983, the Kripalu Yoga Fellowship purchased this 125-acre property called Shadowbrook from the Jesuits. That's when Desai brought his community here. By blending Western psychology with ancient Hindu teachings, Desai was instrumental in developing Kripalu style yoga."

"Is he still around? All I see are pictures of Swami Kripalu."

"In 1994, it was discovered Desai was involved in sexual and financial wrongdoing. Imagine the disillusionment of his disciples who were expected to be celibate. Desai had to resign. Today, Kripalu is an educational center run by a board of trustees. Don't even mention the word *guru*. It still hits a raw nerve."

"When my parents were young, they also believed in gurus," I say.

"Were they into yoga?"

"No," I laugh. "Their gurus were Lenin, Stalin, and Mao. Their world collapsed when their gurus betrayed them."

"What happened after that?"

"That's a conversation for another time."

Joy's final words stun me as we enter the Shadowbrook Room. "You know," she says, stopping for a meaningful pause, "our instructor Yoganand was Desai's closest disciple."

21: *Metamorphosis, Stage Two*

Free-spirited and light on my feet, I twirl my way into the Shadowbrook Room, swaying my hips and shoulders to the upbeat Caribbean music. When the music stops, Martha instructs us to use our bodies—without words—to create two sculptures: our shadow fearful side and our optimistic, forceful one. As a person who loves words, I am stumped at how I will get my body to express two such contrasting emotions without the use of language.

My fearful statue is formed by getting down on my knees, folding my trunk forward, and placing my forehead on the floor with shoulders pulled toward each other in a tight grip, my hands clutching my belly. Trapped, I feel vulnerable, unprotected. A dark tunnel appears, and I am in its center, deserted and defenseless with no one to help me. My breathing speeds up, overshadowing my thoughts. My heart pounds, then races. As soon as the instructor tells us to release the pose, the fearful responses leave my body as quickly as air rushing from a balloon. Once the fear is expelled, a sharper reality forms. A new way of thinking brings truth: I can change how I feel and think by changing the way I move or position my body.

In contrast to my fearful sculpture, I am proud, life-affirming, and confident when standing tall, chest wide open, shoulders pulled back, legs grounded, arms spread out like an eagle in flight, head lifted, gaze focused on smiling Shiva. This is the *me* I want to be: strong, centered, complete. These two primeval exercises are undeniable proof of what is presented in the Kripalu manual: my emotions are permanently intertwined with my body's energy circuits.

This firsthand experience also explains why I feel grounded in tree pose when standing on one leg with arms steepled overhead, protected in child pose when curled up in a nurturing ball, and empowered in warrior II pose with legs in a wide lunge and arms reaching out to embrace life. So I must disengage from my mind's tendency to rationalize and assert its will (my biggest downfall!), and for that to happen I need to listen to the messages my body and breath are sending me. I can't wait to tell Joy about what feels like a breakthrough insight.

"In this next exercise," Martha says, dividing us into groups of five, "you will be sitting in an interlocked chain. The first person, the receiver, will lean into the givers for support. You'll be changing roles so everybody has a chance to be both a receiver and a giver."

When last in the chain of interlocked bodies, both my arms are wrapped tightly around the waist of the person in front of me. "Lean into me. I have you. Let go," I reassure her.

The roles are now reversed, and I am first in line, a receiver. As soon as I lean back, my body stiffens, and my hands frantically look for something to hold onto. Sweat beads pop on my forehead, and my legs involuntarily move from a soft shudder to a twitch. My heart beats to the occasion, accelerating to explosion.

I flash to the past. Suddenly, I am eleven years old. My girlfriend Vlasta and I are walking along the frozen Vltava River in search of treasures. Without realizing how far we have wandered, we hear the ice underneath us crack open. Our waterlogged clothing pulls us into the water. A man comes to our rescue when he hears us scream *pomoc, pomoc* (help). Strangers take us wet, shivering, and scared into their house. After stripping off our wet clothes, they wrap us in blankets, give us warm tea with honey, and call our mothers. Belle's gestures and facial expressions of gratitude compensate for her poor Czech. Leaning into the bodies behind me makes me feel the same helplessness I felt the day I was sinking into the freezing waters of the Vltava River.

Back to the present, I awake as receiver. My mind enters the bleak zone. "I'm sinking! Help! Let me sit up. I'm drowning." My arms flail aimlessly. My body and voice are weak.

The person behind me whispers, "We have you, Ann. You're okay."

"I, I, I can't, *please,* let me go." With a swift movement, I press my elbows into the person behind me to jerk my body out of her embrace.

"What happened? Why were you so frantic?" Joy's attention pitches a lifeline to my fragile state.

"I felt I was falling into a deep hole."

"Was it that bad? Is there some history to this?" Joy asks, her brown eyes searching mine for answers.

I relay the story of my near drowning. "It felt like I was sinking deeper and deeper." I shiver, brushing the memory away. "Do you believe the body has a memory? Don't our fingers retain a muscular memory of a keyboard we rely on when we type? Something beyond my control made me react that way."

"A sudden sensation or sound can make us relive frightening experiences. It's an involuntary response that happens on a cellular level," Joy explains.

"I tend to push away feelings of sadness and fear. Boy, my body's memory bank must be overflowing with stuff I have not dealt with..." I say, lightening the mood.

"Next time, stay with your sadness and fear. Eventually, new feelings will emerge, and some of them might even be good ones. It's taken me a long, long time to get the message."

"That's a deal, my wise little guru," I say affectionately.

The sound of bamboo flutes tells me it is time to stop thinking. I approach the day's yoga practice with a new respect for my body's means of communication. While on my belly in bow posture, with head and chest lifted, knees bent, and hands reaching for my feet, my thighs, chest, arms, and knees become a chorus singing out the posture's purpose. Imagining myself a conductor of a symphony, I no longer feel my knees crying for a release or my hands struggling to reach my feet. I have become the beauty and power that bring my feet, arms, chest, and lifted head into a harmonious whole, a bow waiting for its arrow to take aim.

When going into down dog, I glance at Joy. Her head is pointing toward her mat with an expression of blissful surrender, her hair swaying as if caressed by a soft breeze. Her heals are grounded on the mat, her legs are stretched out like a meditating heron, and her arms are stretched forward like a yawning cat with its buttocks in the air. She is completely at peace with herself and with what she is doing in the moment. Yoga is in her bloodstream, and the *yamas* and *niyamas* (ethical values of yoga) keep her life on course. Now that I know what hard work it is to get to that stage, I admire what she has accomplished; she is a model to me and others.

Our teachers are right about Swami Kripalu. He knew something about the mystery of our bodies we connect with when we listen to the body's distinctive language. It is humbling to accept that I am better off if I let *my body be my mind's teacher* after a lifetime of believing the intellect knows best.

Postscript

In the last year of my sister's life, I watched her slip into a world beyond my reach. The battle with Alzheimer's was lost long before the disease ended her life. Though she did not recognize my husband, remember she once had a husband of fifty years, or recall the house she refused to leave until she lost her cognizance of where she was, she never forgot who I was. Whenever I showed up in the Cambridge care home, she would smile sweetly, and without knowing why I was there or where I came from, she would reach her arms out, and in a happy, girlish voice and eyes melting with love, she would say, "My baby sister. My baby sister."

She stopped speaking English when the end was near. This brief return of hers to the non-Alzheimer's stage of life she had once lived in Czech was a balm for my aching soul. For Czech was the language that bound us to each other. The spontaneous eruption of the words *moje sestřička* (my baby sister) she so lovingly repeated was still on her lips when her breath left her body. Unlike the mind, the body expresses through gesture, smile, the press of the hand, the blink of an eye, or the spontaneous outpouring of uncensored words the bare truth that gives life its most profound meaning.

For me, yoga postures act as a golden thread that weaves the memory of what I have lived to what I am currently living, the way Laura's memory of her *baby sestřička* lived on in her shattered memory despite everything else Alzheimer's had taken from her.

22: *Stage Three, Larva*

"What happened to Yoganand after he learned about Desai's betrayal?" I ask Joy on our walk to Lake Mahkeenac.

"After Desai resigned, Yoganand left Kripalu to sort things out. Now a highly respected master, he carries on the Kripalu traditions."

"I know how hard it is to rebuild your life after being disillusioned by somebody or something you fervently believed in. Do you think yoga helped him through his crisis?"

"Possibly. Has yoga helped you come to terms with your past?"

"My mental dramas get played out during my yoga practices. It's a constant process of discovery. My reactions to the postures help me understand the way I behave when I am not on the yoga mat. I recently read that the ancient yogis used meditation to connect with a higher spirit and to grapple with their destructive behavior patterns. It's good to know I'm not the only one who needs help to keep myself together."

"You can add me to that list," Joy says with a laugh. "Yoga helps me balance the material world I live in with the spiritual one I want to practice in my everyday life. There are so many things at my job that go against my personal philosophy."

"How do you deal with the frustration of that divide?"

"I control what I can: I'm a vegetarian, though my husband is not, I do yoga and I meditate, and he does not, and I strive to be truthful and compassionate with people on the job, even when they scheme behind my back."

"You're making a mark on the world—a statement of strength. I'm still working on improving the quality of my yoga practices. And I haven't even considered meditation yet. Before I can be a model to others, like you, I must sort myself out first."

"Let's be grateful the spiritual practices of the ancient yogis paved the way for the rest of us on the path of self-improvement," Joy says with a smile in her voice.

The continuous question is how we live versus how we want to be living. The conversations at meals include new realizations and insights, which are parlayed back and forth during breaks and between classes. At nighttime, if someone shares a juicy thought, it bounces from person to person like a tossed volleyball. There's Kathy, a massage therapist cognizant of the body's secrets; Rachel, an herbalist whose expertise heals wounds; Robert, a teacher at an Iyengar studio; and Joy, who studied with some of the best yoga teachers in the nation—each one expands my knowledge of yoga's potential to restore, revive, and heal.

Kripalu is a protective womb in which we share stories about our lives we don't usually discuss in the outside world.

Ethical principles of yoga explored in the morning lecture generate multiple conversations. Jody, a kindergarten teacher with a short bob and oversized purple frames that draw attention to her friendly face, laments in her distinctive New York accent, "The guidelines for *truthfulness in speech and action* sent a message I needed to hear. I've been dishonest about my feelings with my boyfriend. How do I tell him I no longer love him? It's not right to pretend. Telling the truth is harder, but it will make me feel better."

Roberta, a travel agent, chimes in. "My husband ridicules my yoga practice. To avoid getting upset, I practice behind his back. I must let him know how much this stresses me out—after all, yoga should be my calm oasis."

Joan, a marketing firm executive in charge of EEO (Equal Employment Opportunity) at her company, complains, "Our toxic office atmosphere dampens my spirits. I'm resolved to do something about it as soon as I get back." Her voice reflects her determination.

Sharon, a curly-haired young woman who works in a dental office, shares her frustrations. "I run the household and cook the meals, plus I have a demanding job! There's no time for *me*." She waves a fist at phantom ghosts to emphasize her protest.

"A colleague asked me for feedback on his 400-page novel." I pause to catch my breath. "Did I say *no*? Was I honest about how late I stay up to get my own work done? Instead, when reading it, I was angry at myself for taking it on."

"To live a meaningful life, we must be honest with ourselves about our emotional needs and limits. Kripalu is helping me see the kind of changes I want to make in my own life. But look!" says Jody, waving us toward the door. "What would Yoganand say if we didn't get to our afternoon practice on time?"

To soothe our tired muscles, Joy and I take a luxurious soak in the hot tub before dinner. "You know," I say, breaking through her reverie, "I can't get Shiva's dance of destruction and creation out of my mind." Swishing my feet in the swirling water, I chant, "Destruction and creation, a unifying dance of opposites," as sprays of hot water wash away the last remnants of muscle tightness in my shoulders.

Joy suddenly perks up. "I get it. There's a dance of opposites waltzing inside you, and you can't name it yet."

Reaching for my towel, I say, "Actually, I just understood why Shiva is so joyful—he's dancing a victory dance over his destructive impulses. That would make me happy too." I wrap the towel around my shoulders, pleased with my insight.

During a quiet walk on the Kripalu grounds, I reflect on my recent victory over my lifelong addiction to coffee and how that fits in with Shiva's victory dance. In Prague, I drank dark, thick, fragrant Turkish coffee served on a silver tray with a demitasse cup and a stainless-steel pot with a long handle and narrow neck.

In America, I drank mugs of coffee with cream. In Montreal, I fell in love with bowls of café au lait. Coffee fueled conversations with friends and deepened my absorption in a book. I loved everything about it, from its taste and penetrating aroma to the surge of energy it sent through me.

However, this is what I chose to overlook: the third cup that has a stale, muddy taste; the stomach cramps and hyped-up feeling from an overdose of caffeine; and the headache if I couldn't get my caffeine fix. I asked myself—what am I going to do about it? If awareness is the backbone of yoga, then why don't I act on it? When high on my yoga practice, why would I need a coffee high? A gnawing thought persisted: maybe it was time to quit.

Once the withdrawal symptoms passed, my body movements were less impulsive, my gaze less restless, my chest lighter, my stomach more relaxed, and my mind less jumpy. No longer dependent on a cup of coffee to push through a batch of papers, I either take a walk, do a few stretches, or give in to a short nap when I am tired. Quitting coffee strengthened my resolve to say no to other things that were not good for me, like giving in to the pressure to read a colleague's work when I don't have the time to do it.

Strolling the Kripalu grounds, I feel the power of nature's changing cycles, which parallel my change from a non-yoga person to a yogini, a coffee drinker to an herbal tea drinker, a yoga student to a yoga teacher. Change is happening in me and around me. Is my farewell to coffee that different from the dormant trees changing into leaf-covered beauties in the spring?

The intellectually charged Kripalu atmosphere of self-examination prompts me to question my own truth about how I want to live and how I will make it happen. In this removal from the pressures and obligations of daily life, I am more aware of how the choices I make affect how I feel about

myself. Awareness that something is not quite right is the starting point of change. *Questioning, probing, changing*—these
words get replayed in my head as I commune with Shiva, who
dares me to lift my legs high enough to not get burned when
dancing over life's hot flames. And here, in the company of my
fellow searchers, I am preparing myself to take on that challenge.

23: *From Chrysalis to Butterfly*

Before our 6:00 a.m. yoga practice, I make my way through the quiet hallways to the dimly lit dining room for a cup of herbal tea. I can barely discern from the window in the Silent Dining Room the outline of the mountains that look like two camel humps. I wrap my fingers around the paper cup to absorb its warmth while fresh impressions about my Kripalu experiences are running through my head like a newsreel. Though the factual knowledge about the postures is important, my responses to the postures tell me about myself—if I'm accepting of my physical limitations, why some postures frustrate me, and how exciting it is to become aware of parts of my body previously ignored like my kidneys and sacrum. I am learning about my attitudes when I listen to the language of my sensations and finding the link between the mental activity of my mind, my movements, and my breath. I trust the postures to lead me out of ambiguity and doubt and point me toward self knowledge and aliveness the way a compass might get me out of a labyrinth.

Throughout the day, I am either practicing yoga postures or studying, writing, talking, or reading about them. Like people, each posture has a different personality and mood. For instance, the triangle posture is both grounding with my legs firmly planted and a release when my chest expands and my arms stretch in two directions. When in the posture, I feel an uplifting sense of wonder and adventure; when I come out of it, I am focused and happy. If I'm lethargic when going into the triangle, it revives me; if sad or anxious, it comforts me. If I think of my yoga mat as my working laboratory, the Kripalu shop is my study hall.

Here, I learn about the differences between Iyengar, Ashtanga, Anusara, Kundalini, Sivananda, Bikram, Integral, and Kripalu schools of yoga. I peruse books of Rumi's poetry, the *Bhagavad Gita*, meditation guides, books about yoga therapy and philosophy, and personal stories about how yoga changed, improved, or redirected people's lives. I reach for a book with a title that sends my head spinning, *Yoga and the Quest for the True Self* by Stephen Cope, Kripalu scholar-in-residence. *This is the guy I had my first Kripalu yoga class with!* I sprint to the cash register, and tucking my find in my bag, I dash up to the phone booth on the third floor to call Dennis.

"I'm learning so much!" I tell him. "Yoga is so much more than having a practice, it's…"

"You sound fired up."

"I'm in awe of what a complex mechanism the body is. By the way, I bought a book on finding your true self that might explain what I am searching for. I love you! Class is about to start. Hugs."

Back in the Shadowbrook Room, I lengthen, hold, and release my breath in Yoganand's advanced breathing techniques
class. Sounding like a locomotive pushing up a steep hill, my
rapid breaths claim my full attention.

"Focus your awareness on your belly. Drop into your center. Hold your breath until the need for breath is strong. Dissolve. Watch. Feel." Yoganand's compelling voice comes in
waves that complement the oceanic sounds of my breath. An
unexpected lightness floods my body as if a big windshield
wiper has cleared out my mind's content. "Slow down your
breath. Open your eyes." Yoganand brings our journey into
space to a close.

Pulled out of the ordinary and into the exalted, my mind
is emptied, as if movers cleared out all the furniture for a new
tenant. My index finger and thumb move toward my thigh.
The pinch confirms I am still here. Did the exercise last a few
minutes? An hour? How did Yoganand use the breath to alter
the state of my mind so quickly? It's another one of those yoga
mysteries I hope to unravel, but for now, I trust myself to follow
Yoganand into untried possibilities.

With eyes closed and a tender expression lighting up his
face, Yoganand sinks into easy pose. The buzz in the room
quiets. Sixty sets of eyes are glued to his still body. As if waking from a dream, he stands up, and parting his legs in a wide
lunge, he extends his arms like wings, head high, chest puffed
out. Fleeting emotions of sadness, joy, and introspection cross
his face with the speed of lightning. His gaze, like a laser fixed
on a spot in the distance, reminds me of Abe pacing back and

forth oblivious to what is going on around him while thinking through a phrase or an idea. Yoganand's medium of expression is the body, while Abe's was the written word. This haunting presentation of warrior II brings the wisdom of the ancient yogis into the present and into my own body.

Yoganand lowers his arms. His legs slowly move toward each other until he is back in mountain pose, his starting position. He waits before he asks us to put into words what this posture made us *feel*. Our impressions are vocalized: grace, strength, self-reliance, power, beauty, contemplation, the song of a free spirit, *reverence*. Where did this power to express one's deepest feelings come from? Do I also have it? The message is clear—each posture is a story, and I am the creator of its narrative. The posture is merely a suggestion for me to express my own story, which changes day by day.

On a cold January afternoon, Martha sends us out to find a tree we like on the Kripalu grounds. "Spend time with your tree. Study it. Create a story about it and then return to the Shadowbrook Room," she instructs us with an enigmatic smile.

I run down a steep hill to befriend the tall, lone evergreen with well-proportioned branches. The wide bottom branches form a perfect shelter for rabbits, squirrels, and birds. Near the top of the tree, the branches get smaller and smaller until the tree narrows to a single shoot at the very top. Symmetry and balance meet and marry. Newly sprouted light green pine needles at the tips of the branches contrast with the more established dark green ones. The more I look at the tree, the more I notice. The more I notice, the stronger my connection is to the tree.

Back in the Shadowbrook Room, soft music and the glow of lit candles invite me to snuggle into my cushion while, with pen in hand, I speak to my tree: "I stand motionless in front of you, awestruck by your beauty and regal presence. I want to crawl under your lower branches, where I will be sheltered from the January winds and snow. I admire the flirtatious sway of your branches when you address me. 'I am strong. I've been here for generations. My roots are firmly established so that no storm or blizzard can harm me. I have brought joy to others with my beautiful presence. Caress the soft shoots of my beautiful children at the tips of my branches. I welcome you to my home.'

"Like you, I am growing stronger roots to weather life's storms, and I have baby sprouts of my own that are coming to life in me."

I am not the same person who arrived at Kripalu nine days ago when I board the Greyhound bus for the trip home. Profound yoga practices, exposure to new concepts and ways of thinking, relationships with seasoned yoga practitioners, and the ability to communicate with my body on more intimate terms have given me a new set of lenses.

Once home, I jump into Dennis's arms, fastening my legs around his waist, almost knocking him over. "What an experience!" I shout and laugh at the same time. "Look, I brought my yoga practice to new heights." Dropping to my knees, I lift my hips and straighten my legs, then pose into down dog.

Dennis and Daniel, who lifts his head up from his piano playing, clap. "Impressive!" Dennis exclaims. "What else did you study?"

"Anatomy, teaching methods, the communication channels between the body and the mind, *nadis*, which are channels for energy to move through the body—"

Dennis holds up his hand. "You've already lost me."

"At first I felt like I landed in a land where they spoke a foreign language. But my friend Joy is changing that."

"You'll tell us about her at dinner. For now, are you ready for a glass of wine?"

"Meat, coffee, and wine never crossed my mind. Amazing!"

"Okay, your mind was on higher things. Time to get back and enjoy what I prepared for you," he says, handing me a glass of white wine.

Static electricity crackles under my feet as I whirl around the living room to the sounds of the Beethoven sonata Daniel is playing in the background.

Dennis lifts his glass. "A toast to the new AK!"

"Is that me?"

"Yes. *K* for Kripalu! Do you think AK is up for some spicy chicken?"

Aromas pull me toward the food, and my grumbling stomach telegraphs my hunger. Between bites, I describe the emotional connection I made with Joy. "She's a walking yoga encyclopedia. She loves traveling to exotic places, cats, and introducing people to yoga. Her laugh is just like her name, joyful."

"You're lucky you found somebody like that."

"True. But enough about me. What's new at work? Have you heard from Michael? And your mother, how is she?"

"Nothing new, but we'll get to that later. I want to know what brought you back home in such an ecstatic state."

"I wish I could explain. I feel like I've grown butterfly wings. All those profound practices and exercises unblocked something in me. And my understanding of the human body has completely changed. Perhaps by the end of the training, I'll understand this profusion of aliveness."

In my spare time, I study my Kripalu manual, read the books I bought at the Kripalu shop, practice yoga, and record my observations and thoughts in my journal.

"Joy," I shout into the telephone, "I'm making incredible progress in my practices."

"I'm all ears," she cheers.

"I've realized that when I leave my will out of it, my postures come with so much more ease."

"That's what Patanjali says in the *Yoga Sutras*: go into the postures with steadiness and ease. That's the Kripalu spirit! Can't wait for Session II and meeting up again!"

On my way to teach a literature class on Tolstoy's story *The Death of Ivan Ilyich,* I notice my shoulders are scrunched and my shoes feel like bricks. My mind is flittering from what I will cook for dinner to Daniel's need for a new coat to when I can get over to the fitness center for a swim. Instinctively, I recite the five Kripalu principles to bring myself into the present moment: breathe, relax, feel, watch, allow. I stop to look up at the floating clouds. I take a few deep, unrushed breaths. The compression in my chest lets up, my face relaxes, and the tightness in my shoulders and neck eases. Energy finds its life source and surges from my mind to my heart, reviving my sagging spirit and body. My thoughts return to Tolstoy, and along with it, the excitement I felt when developing my analysis for today's class.

"Good afternoon," I begin. "Look at the sun casting a radiance on the silvery leaves of the crab apple tree under our window." I pause to give the students time to take it in. "For Tolstoy, nature was a means of connecting with God's universe and the mystery of life. Which character in *The Death of Ivan Ilyich* is closest to God? What effect does this have on Ivan Ilyich?"

Numerous hands go up. What follows is a lively debate about Ivan Ilyich's values and his realization about life's true meaning minutes before his death. For a moment, everything comes together: the shimmering light of the crab apple tree; my deep absorption in Tolstoy's story; the students' engagement in Ivan Ilyich's plight; and the principles of yoga I am bringing into my life.

When I breathe, relax, feel, watch, and allow, my quest for fulfillment and wholeness begins.

24: *All Is Within Me*

When I return for Session II in April, familiar whiffs of incense from the Kripalu shop tickle my nose and bouquets of Indian curry spices waft from the kitchen, waking memories of hunger and satiety in past Kripalu culinary experiences. The poignant yoga quotations along the wall pull past enlightenments and profound insights into the way my body works into the present. Having shed their winter attire, the Berkshire Hills are putting on their spring clothing. The air is full of the excitement of a new season, and I am anticipating meeting up with my fellow trainees who, except for Joy, have been put on hold for the last three months.

"Hello, Shiva dear, I'm back," I murmur, feeling as though I am meeting a family member after a long separation. I swear he nods back at me. Not to hurt the skeleton's feelings, I wink at it.

I reclaim my bed under the window with its prime view of the starlit sky. Plunking my suitcase on the floor and flopping on the bed to enjoy the view, I place my arms around my shoulders and give myself a welcome hug. "I belong."

Boom, thud, crash, bang. Doors keep opening and closing with each arrival. I turn back to the room. Floodgates open as old friends stampede in. There are thumps of luggage dropped on the floor, shouts, bear hugs, and many voices at once: "How are you?" "Your hair is longer!" "Love your yoga shirt." "Have you lost weight?"

Joy shouts, "Ann! Over here." She moves to one side, passes a person, jumps up to wave at me, then moves aside and goes around another. Finally, she makes her way through the throng and grabs my shoulders and hugs me, rocking me back and forth. "*So* glad to see you!" she yells over the din.

"Me too! I like your new hairdo. Ready for afternoon yoga in the Forest Room?" I ask as I fling my yoga bag over my shoulder. "It's tradition!" I sing "Tradition" from *Fiddler on the Roof* in a high-pitched voice.

Once again, our affirmations are posted on the wall behind Shiva. Mine reads: "Personal Enrichment, Improved Mastery of the Self, Self-discovery." Hmm, *self-discovery,* like Christopher Columbus about to discover the New World! My yoga mat has become a ship on which I navigate between my head and heart on this adrenaline-charged pilgrimage into myself.

In his welcoming lecture, Yoganand makes a distinction between experience, which is the here and the now, and storytelling, which is masterminded in our head. He describes the ongoing battle between our heart, or sensations, and our intellect that spins stories about who we are. To distinguish between the real and the fictional, we must know what we feel. I decide that my challenge for this session is to avoid distancing from my feelings. Can I do it?

The sun caresses my back as I prepare my first twenty-five-minute teaching practice at a picnic table on the Kripalu grounds. My assignment is to develop a centering, introduce an intention, select appropriate warm-ups for warrior I, and close with a final centering. Frisky chickadees hop around while I transfer information about the postures to index cards. Addressing the birds, bugs, and butterflies, I read: "Warrior I develops concentration, coordination, balance and poise, strength and groundedness…" The chickadees seem happy with my explanation of why warrior I is such a terrific posture.

But my stomach twists in knots at the prospect of facing my very first yoga students, even if they are only my fellow trainees, and at having my performance evaluated. Will I remember to mention when to inhale and exhale, list each benefit and counter-indication, get the tempo and transitions just right? *How do I get them to love the postures?* Sweat gathers in beads on my forehead. My hand shakes when I rewrite my cues on a new set of index cards. My brain freezes. *Am I meant to be a yoga teacher?*

Heavy tension permeates the Shadowbrook Room on the morning of our exam. Bleary-eyed and rattled, I go over my lesson plan one last time before it is my turn to teach. *Breathe in, hold for four counts, breath out for four.* Slowly, my lost confidence seeps back when I see my group of eight smiling students waiting to be instructed. However, my shaky voice lacks conviction, and too scared I will get something wrong, I regurgitate the descriptions I memorized from the manual. Though lacking color or vibrancy, my instructions work. *Okay, I can do this!* says the voice in my head. My demeanor relaxes, and my sense of humor returns as soon as I depart from the wording in the manual. "Now, like a dog at a fire hydrant, lift your right leg in the air," I tell my students, happy to hear their snickering. Reassured, I get through the remaining minutes of my presentation with no mishaps.

"Dennis!" I say, pressing the telephone receiver to my ear. "I still sound like the manual, but I got through the exam with no major glitches. I must develop a voice of my own. And trust it. Hmm, how interesting, 'trust in myself' is what I wrote as my intention for this session."

"Good going! You're charging forward like a steam engine."

"Off to see how the others are teaching. Love from your *almost* yoga teacher." A giggle explodes from my lips at the image of myself as an *almost* yoga teacher.

A few days later, during deep relaxation in Michael's practice teach class, the Czech word *najdeš* bursts forth, then it quickly recedes. Like a blinking neon sign, *najdeš* flashes back before Michael brings us out of deep relaxation. Caught in a dreamlike haze, I wonder if this is a message, and if so, what it might be.

During feedback time, I tell the class about the sudden appearance of the word *najdeš*. "I'm proficient in Czech because I spent my childhood in Prague," I explain. "*Najdeš* means 'you will find.' So what," I query, "do I need to find?"

My classmates look puzzled. For an explanation, they look to Michael, then at Tarika, a Kripalu staff instructor evaluating his performance. Focusing on me, she speculates, "Your mind evidently reverted back to your childhood when Czech was your primary language. The meaning of this occurrence will most likely come to light when you least expect it."

There is only one person who can help me figure this out.

My fingers trembling, I trip over my words as I shout into the phone, "Dennis, you won't believe what just happened. The word *najdeš* appeared out of the blue, not once, but twice while I was in deep relaxation. It has to be something momentous, don't you think?"

Dennis cuts through my perplexity with his usual acumen. "Maybe your Czech and American selves are finding each other. A bridge between the divide in you?"

"True, my two selves have been living on separate islands. I am either one or the other, which means neither seems complete."

Dennis agrees, "Your Czech self is an important part of who you are. Why do you think I've been working on learning Czech?"

"I always thought it was because of your love of Slavic languages and dialects."

"Yes, that, but more compelling—because it brings me closer to that part of you."

"I'm so touched." My heart swells, and my eyes fill and spill over. "I wish I was there to hug you. Let's speak Czech more often. You're so good at it. You'll help me sort this out. Nobody knows me as well as you do. Right now, I'm on overload. We'll talk more when I get home."

"I wonder what surprises will happen next."

Checking my watch, I jump up. "Have to run. Remember, you're my rock! Love you. *Naschledanou* [Goodbye]."

Najdeš. Najdeš. Najdeš. The word keeps pounding in my head. Am I truly inching toward a merger of the two Anns? Is this what Yoganand means when he talks about the healing properties of breath and movement? Perhaps it welds what is fractured in me. One thing I know for sure: the more I live in the present, the stronger I become.

Near the end of training Session II, Joy and I rummage through a rack of sale outfits at the Kripalu shop. I hold up a pair of blue shorts with a drawstring and a yellow tank top with the letters Y-O-G-A formed with human bodies in yoga postures.

Joy's face lights up. "Try those. It's time to get out of those baggy pants and that floppy T-shirt."

"I'm too self-conscious about my belly to wear something like that."

"Nonsense. How about a new look?" She pushes me toward the dressing room.

A few minutes later, I'm heading toward the cashier.

"You look ten years younger," Joy notes with a smile.

I enter the Shadowbrook Room in my new outfit hoping nobody will notice me. No such luck. "What a nice outfit, Ann. It becomes you," a number of classmates comment as I make my way to my yoga mat in front of my silent friend, the skeleton. At sixty, I am letting myself be the way I am, no more hiding or camouflaging. Calming myself, I let out a sigh. *It's all okay!* After a few gentle warm-ups to test my body in unencumbered movement, I bask in the feel of a *new* Ann.

Martha is preparing us for the next exercise. "Close your eyes. Take a few deep breaths. In the form of an affirmation, answer the following question: What will make you feel complete?"

From nowhere, the phrase *all is within me* pops up. Were these words orchestrated by the same inner force that brought up the word *najdeš* a few days ago? How could I have known that what I was supposed to find was in me all along? That the power to do so *is all within me* but has gone unrecognized. Nothing can describe the happiness I feel at finding the right code to unlock my fiercely guarded private vault. I let the largeness of the moment wrap its arms around me.

With our affirmations set, Martha divides us into two groups: one group sits in a circle with their eyes closed while the other group walks behind them whispering their affirmations: to feel loved, to be in love, to nurture and forgive myself, to be a dancer, to be an artist, to be a yoga teacher, to open my heart, to be in a continuous state of growth, to be joyful, to be fulfilled. Being witness to these outward directed hopes for fulfillment brings tears to my eyes. For I am not seeking completeness in the act of *becoming* but in being what I already am. I repeat "All is within me" like a prayer, a euphoric symphony, an expression of faith in my own power. Session II is far exceeding my intention for personal enrichment, improved mastery of the self, and self-discovery. So far, my voyage into myself has unearthed a treasure box I did not know was there.

I enter the crowded Albany bus station like someone who has forgotten what the world is like outside the protective Kripalu walls. Though everything around me is as it was before, I see it with different eyes. I smile affectionately at the small children playing with matchbox cars and the people munching on snacks and pacing impatiently before the boarding gate. My altered perception transforms what is drab into color, quiet into music, and unsightly into beauty.

On the bus ride, I soak in the rolling hills, cows chewing on grass, children playing in school playgrounds, and dogs roaming through Upstate New York towns. I close my eyes to tone down my energy volume before I review my notes from Yoganand's morning lecture, in which he reminded us, "Shutting out parts of ourselves to avoid pain and hurt not only disconnects us from ourselves but suppresses the aliveness we would feel if we let the full spectrum of our emotions in." His words are resonating deeply: "Opening up to what you feel, be it pleasure, pain, anger, love, or hurt, is the way to feel alive." My heightened aliveness must be a sign of a reconnection to disregarded parts of myself. And to feel is to be alive!

I am home. It is a rainy spring day. Still on a yoga high, I am off to teach Jonathan Franzen's novel *The Corrections* in my Introduction to Fiction class. I feel anything and everything is possible. Wonder quickly turns to concern when I look at my students' blank faces.

Hoping to get a discussion going, I ask, "Why is the Lambert family falling apart? What went wrong?" In vain, I wait for a response. Finally, a few hands go up, but discussion is sluggish. How will I make it to the end of class with forty indifferent students? I despair.

Surprising myself, I give an order. "Everybody, please stand up." They obey. In an authoritative voice, I continue. "Inhale and bring your arms overhead. Exhale as you bring them down into a forward bend." Bewildered, they follow my orders. "Take a few deep breaths with your mouth closed. Let your belly balloon on the inhale." After a few more rounds of inhales and exhales, arm lifts followed by forward bends, and a balancing tree, I let them return to their seats. "Close your eyes to let the energy settle." When they open their eyes, looking more alert and engaged than before, I explain, "I'm training to become a yoga teacher. I thought bringing a bit of energy into our bodies would bring some life into our discussion. Let's see if it works."

The yogis were right. The students pile out of the classroom discussing the disintegration of the Lambert family and similarities with families they know, in some cases even their own. I just taught my *first yoga class,* not yet certified, but fully aware that yoga has the magic to change apathy to engagement. I found the courage to rouse an Introduction to Fiction class with forty lethargic students by acting on my affirmation that *all is within me.* On my way out of the classroom, I expand that affirmation to *all that is within me is in my power.* Would this have happened if yoga hadn't paved the way for me to fulfill this affirmation?

25: Culmination

Finally, the June Session III is here! I have the same dorm room, the same bunk bed, and the same view of the mountains with its luminous sky. Summer beauty is putting on a vibrant show: a blooming crab apple tree with pink and white blossoms and colorful daisies and chrysanthemums compete for attention. Despite my anxiety about the upcoming teaching, I am happy to be back in my yoga home. I know the material and have been fascinated with what I am learning. Just as I let in the worry—do I have what it takes to be a good yoga teacher?—my yoga compatriots begin to fill the room, chattering, high-fiving, and asking, "How are you?" The typical response: "Happy to be back!"

"Are you ready for the teaching?" Rachel, usually withdrawn, asks in a chipper voice.

"If we're to become teachers, we have to plunge in," I say, hoping my voice hides my apprehension.

"It might not be as hard as you think. They've done such a great job preparing us!" Rachel opines.

"My yoga-training high from last April keeps me grounded," Kathryn says, pointing to her mat that it's time for our yoga practice.

On the way to the Forest Room, I recall how I felt the first time I arrived here on that wintry January day six months ago. The newcomers I pass now look as intimidated and disoriented as I felt. In solidarity, I send them a big, friendly smile. Out of breath, but smiling from ear to ear, Joy slips into the Forest Room in time for centering. Reaching out to hug her, I move my mat to make room for her.

"The drive took longer than expected, but I'm here!" she whispers before we close our eyes. And so, Session III is off to a promising start.

Joy and I carry our lunch trays to the picnic table so we can face the sun-covered mountains. Sliced carrots, chunks of broccoli and cauliflower, and sugar snap peas on Bibb lettuce dazzle from our salad bowls. Leaning toward me, Joy notes, "Yoganand and Martha got us right back into an energetic working tempo. What's your focus this session, aside from ac-ing the teaching exam?"

Eager for Joy's input, I confide, "Shiva might agree that my intention to trust, hear, know, and strengthen myself tells me it's time I 'destroy' my dependence on others, particularly my parents. They still have the power to guide my choices."

"What about Dennis? You and he have such different back-grounds. Has his value system influenced you?"

The tree branches gently brush my face as we make our way up a steep hill. "True, Dennis has a strong religious founda-tion and a big clan of relatives he can rely on. His stable roots accentuate my void. I never realized how much I relied on my parents to manage my unorthodox background—that is, until

I lost them." A deep sigh involuntarily interrupts my train of thought. "Dennis is very understanding, but I have to define my own value system that is not a replica of my parents' or a submission to what works for him."

"How do you think you will do that?"

"My passion for yoga! Yoga has turned me into a detective. I am out to discover who I really am independent of these outside forces. Those brief moments when I don't feel torn are precious. But enough about me," I interrupt myself. "Has the Kripalu training made a difference in how you feel about yourself?"

"I'm definitely less judgmental about past mistakes. For years, I've struggled with a complicated relationship with my mother. Changing my attitude about our differences has made it easier to see her good qualities. Hey, don't underestimate the importance of compassion and acceptance. It sure beats waiting for things to be what they are not and most likely never will be. So yes, Kripalu is showing me the way."

"Doesn't a compassionate attitude help heal past wounds?"

"True. And you're well on your way." Joy picks up a small, shiny rock and puts it in my hand. Staring in my eyes, she says, "This rock is to remember how much we've grown at Kripalu. I liken this experience to a speedboat taking us to new places, new vistas, new heights. And I'm loving the ride!"

"Oops, it's time for our presentation. Philosophizing is over." I grab Joy's hand as we run down the hill screaming, "Here we come!" Hoping nobody notices we are a few minutes late, we quietly slip into the Shadowbrook Room for another dose of yoga wisdom.

Already seated in lotus pose in the center of the room with his eyes closed, Yoganand looks like a perfectly carved statue. Soft overhead lighting illuminates his peaceful face. The American Indian music of Peter Kater and R. Carlos Nakai's album *Migration* builds a sense of mystery and anticipation about Kripalu Stage III yoga, a meditation in motion where prana (life force) moves the body. Yoganand starts out with subtle movements that grow in complexity and expressiveness. With eyes focused above our heads, his body narrates the tension between the polarities of strength and weakness, compassion and detachment, and optimism and hopelessness. The unstructured movements of his arms, legs, and torso personify the short-lived existence of these emotions through a smile, or in counterpoint, an expression of pain followed by calm. These rapidly changing stories of his inward journey conjure my own body's narrative that is craving expression.

Yoganand's movements cycle through sadness, joy, fear, strength, discord, and harmony. He lowers his head like a humble monk in prayer, opens his chest like a proud peacock showing off its feathers, extends his arms like a seagull in flight, anchors his legs like marble pillars, and focuses his eyes like a wise owl. *What would these spontaneous movements reveal about me?* When Yoganand's journey is over, he returns to his statuesque form. Witnessing this staging of what makes us human brings tears to my eyes.

Now it is our turn to try Stage III yoga.

I feel like an actress on opening night. Dimmed lights encourage me to turn inward. My eyes are closed. Without moving,

I wait for a response from within. The music's exotic sounds transport me to an open landscape that blends with the scent of freshly cut grass coming through the open windows. Without knowing what I will do, I feel myself placing my right knee between my hands and extending my left leg toward the back of my mat. My chest and head high, I close my eyes, letting my body find its way. As my body takes over, the impossible happens: my torso upright, my right hand reaching for the ankle of the left leg, an inner force overrides my mind's assessment of my limit. Holding my foot in my hand, my spine arched and head tilted back, I am sustained by dare and strength. Miraculously, I am in a variation of pigeon I never believed I could do. Surrendering to the beauty of just being, I fold onto the blanket in a soft heap.

Desire is gone, hunger is absent. I have no wants. I have been emptied out as if someone (was it me?) has taken me apart and put me back together in a new configuration. Fearful of losing that other-earthly sense that I have landed on an unexplored planet, I move toward the door with great care when it is time for our break. Sixty of us pour out of the Shadowbrook Room in a unifying silence. The sunlit patio invites us to decompress in the soft summer air. My arms folded around me, I am proud of the new *me* that is emerging.

"So," I ask Joy later that day over colorful plates of food, "what was Stage III yoga like for you?"

"It was like an explosion of liberated energy flowing through me as freely as the wind."

"Momentous! I felt I was dancing with Shiva."

"I'm struck by how yoga gives each person the right healing balm or the right recipe for reaching their potential."

"Yoga has the magic *we need*. If I can stretch the limits of what I thought I was able to do in Stage III yoga, I can do it in my work and in my relationships. This opens me to a whole new horizon."

Compelled to dissect the postures I plan to teach on my final exam, I study wherever I can—on my bed, on the staircase, in empty yoga practice rooms, and in quiet spots on the Kripalu grounds. The day before the exam that determines if we get certified, we gather in groups of eight to go over the postures in our manual. When it is my turn to demo triangle, my mind is a sudden blank. Wordless, I mumble something in a voice as thin as my self-confidence. A maze of detailed information about the posture's benefits and their counter-indications is making it impossible to access the crucial information about how to get into the posture.

A junior instructor, Christie, notices my struggle. "Ann, you already know what's in the manual. Convey your knowledge through what you are feeling in your body."

"Put your right hand down. Left arm lifts. Look up." Displeased with my performance, I stop.

Christie's expression tells me my delivery is lifeless. "Your wording is stiff, bookish," she says, reinforcing my observation. "Use images to engage others in their own experience."

I understand what Christie wants, but I am too rattled to find the right words. Christie advises, "What are you feeling in the triangle right now? Name it."

Abandoning my notes, I dig into my body to extract the narrative. "Move your right hip back to make room to extend your spine. Feel the elegance of that glide when you open your arms like a bird in flight. Turn your gaze toward the sky."

"That's it! I feel the posture's spirit!"

"Wow, my love for triangle came through this time. It's simpler than I was making it."

With her hand on my shoulder, Christie nods. "And now onto the next posture. Remember, the narrative is in your own body, not in your head."

That evening, I seclude myself in the Mountain Room to go through my lesson plan without my notes. I start with mountain pose. First in my head, then in a whisper, and finally in a strong voice, I articulate what I am feeling in my body as I go in and out of each posture. My mountain blossoms as soon as I lengthen my spine and open my chest and pull my shoulders back. With my feet pressing into the mat and my arms reaching toward the ceiling, I am complete, calm, and balanced. *This is the essence of mountain. This is what mountain is all about.*

When focused on the feel of the posture, I forget about the memorized text from the manual. The more I trust my own wording, the more imaginative I become. Exhilarated, like a helium balloon that has been set free, I float up the stairs to my dorm shocked to realize I practiced for three hours without a break.

Before drifting off to sleep, I bolt upright. Epiphany! *I get it. I get it.* To convey my love for the postures, I must use words that express their spirit the way a musician transposes notes into melody, a painter turns color and form into a painting, or a sculptor chisels stone into a statue. Who would ever think that teaching yoga is an art like writing and poetry that uses words to transform experiences into profound meanings?

The morning of our test announces itself with a flood of light through my window. Back in the Shadowbrook Room, my heart leaps when I see that Martha is my designated evaluator. She is the model of the yoga teacher I want to be: comfortable with herself, reassuring, and passionate about yoga. Once I start teaching, my accelerated breath slows and my clenched hands relax. A comforting smile illuminates Martha's face as I deliver my prompts in a clear, self-assured voice.

Time passes. Although my brain is saturated with theoretical knowledge, it is my heart that carries me through the test. Submitting to my body's knowledge rather than my intellect, I find this to be one of the most difficult (and liberating) tests I have ever taken. I am certain of the results of my evaluation before Martha speaks. As soon as my test is over, Martha wraps her arms around my shoulders, and with her eyes aglow, she whispers, "I loved it!"

"Now I know that to be a credible yoga teacher, I have to integrate the postures into myself. Thank you for teaching me how to do that."

Only I know how many obstacles I had to overcome for this moment to happen.

"I don't know what's happening, Ann, but I can see it's cosmic. You look like you're on your way to your first date," says our assistant Lori, humoring me on the eve of our graduation ceremony.

At a loss for words, I press my hands to my heart.

"You don't have to say anything. I can see that teaching yoga is your calling. I am so happy for you!"

The night sky twinkles and blinks for me for the last time. I have the heart of a sixteen-year-old in a sixty-year-old body. Nothing seems impossible. Too excited to sleep, I quietly sneak down to the Mountain Room as soon as the early morning birds start chattering. Glimmers of light are seeping into the room by the time I complete my warm-ups. As I prepare to go into a lunge, I hear the door open. In the semidarkness, I recognize Joy. We move from posture to posture, each abiding by the dictates of our individual bodies, in celebration of our friendship, which has carried us through the roller-coaster ride of these last months. As 6:00 a.m. approaches, we hug, and with a lump in my throat, I take one last look at the view of the Kripalu grounds shining brightly in the early morning sun.

The dorm room is in a frenzy of graduation preparations. Dressed in white dresses, my classmates are arranging their hair and searching for long-forgotten lipsticks. Up to now, I have only seen them in yoga clothes or pajamas. Do we really look like this in our other lives? When we reach the Shadowbrook Room doors, our animated chatter instantly evaporates.

The festive mood grows dignified as we form a path from the entrance to the podium, where our instructors are waiting to receive us. I walk down the aisle as if I am in a slow-motion movie, my heart singing, my stride feathery, my face beaming. Like proud parents sending a child into the world, Yoganand hands me a raw chickpea, a reminder that personal growth starts with a single seed, and Martha hands me my diploma. Bowing to the smiling faces around me, I practically fly to the back of the line. I scan the room in which I discovered that what I was looking for was in me all along. Would I have found it without the teachings of Swami Kripalu, who came into my life the first day I walked through the Kripalu doors?

Now, trained to bring yoga to others, a new chapter of my life is about to begin.

Part IV:

From Seed to Bloom —Growing Roots

"According to yoga, the purpose of the whole
of creation is to give us a context for understanding
what we are and what we are not."
—T.K.V. Desikachar, *The Heart
of Yoga: Developing a Personal Practice*

26: My First Teaching Job

There it is, hanging above my desk in a soft blue frame.

Kripalu Yoga Teacher Training, Basic Certification, June 23, 2002. Signed, Martha Abbot and Yoganand Michael Carroll.

Unconditional. Unquestionable. Undeniable! I am certified to teach yoga.

But first I must find a place to do that. I'm not optimistic about my chances since it is midsummer in Plattsburgh, vacation season. The town is quiet, almost on hold waiting for the fall for life to begin again. But a phone call out of the blue turns the world around. It's Lilian, the one who told me about Kripalu at a recent dinner party, passing on information about an opening to teach yoga at Plattsburgh's fitness center she cannot fit into her schedule. Scared, but trembling with excitement, I dial the number for the director.

Peter is a young man with the muscles of a body builder, a long blond ponytail, and a shy, sweet smile. I'm sure now that when he sees how old I am, I'll never be hired. After a tour of the facility, we end up in the spacious aerobics room equipped with mats, blocks, and a sophisticated stereo system. He takes my breath away when he says, "This is where you'll have your yoga class. Can you begin next week?"

Thrilled to have the offer but petrified of taking on the role of a yoga teacher so suddenly, I hesitate. "So soon?"

Sensing my confusion, Peter says, "You'll do a great job! Let's fill out the paperwork and get you on the payroll. The previous instructor quit unexpectedly. Our regulars are eager to get back to yoga."

With my contract in hand, I drive down familiar Route 3, as if seeing it anew. I dash into the house yelling, "Dennis, Dennis! I have a job teaching yoga!"

"Wow, that didn't take long. And in one of the largest fitness centers, no less." Dennis's head bobs with approval. "Tonight, we celebrate that there's a yoga teacher in the house! Here she comes!" he says, throwing his arms around me.

"The previous teacher was a *young* woman who quit because of a family problem. I can't help wondering how the students will react to a white-haired lady taking her place."

"You'll show them what 'old' ladies can do. Besides, you have a youthful spirit. Your love of yoga will certainly come through once you get the hang of it."

"Actually," I say, kicking up my heels to one side, "yoga makes me feel young again. My challenge is to show them how ageless yoga is."

Leaving nothing to chance, I map out every detail for my first class. I select my warm-ups, design a balanced posture sequence, and choose a special poem for final centering. I sew a velour pouch for the chime I purchased at the Kripalu shop, select Todd Norian's exotic CD *Bija,* and pick out my favorite navy-blue yoga outfit. The night before the class, I toss and turn, going over my narrative the way I did before my teaching exam.

My knuckles white from the tight grip on the steering wheel and my mind racing faster than the speed limit, I whisper Yoganand's advice about teaching our first class: "Keep it simple." Silently at first, and then like a mantra, with increased force, I repeat, "Keep it simple. Keep it simple. Okay, I get it, but *how* do I keep it simple?" Entering the aerobics room, I run my fingers over the locket with the chickpea Yoganand gave me at graduation. *Remember, all is within me,* I remind myself, returning to the moment those magical words changed my way of thinking.

The garish sign of the Consumer Square Plaza with its list of store names, visible from the aerobics room window, affects my ability to create a Kripalu-like atmosphere. Traffic noise, car fumes, and the smell of fried food from a fast-food joint seep in through the open window. The swaying traffic light is nothing like the tall trees outside the Kripalu Forest Room. I shut the window to block out the noise and nauseating odors. I put on Norian's CD and spread mats, blocks, blankets, and straps around the room. As students start trickling in, I resort to my breath to keep myself steady and calm.

"Hi! My name is Ann," I say in an uncharacteristically thin voice once the students are settled. *Can they sense my inexperience and tentativeness?* Pausing to steady my nerves, I explain, "I'm trained in Kripalu yoga."

A blond woman in the back of the room shrugs her shoulders. "*Kripalu* yoga? Never heard of that."

A shiver ripples up my spine. *Can I pull this off?*

"Kripalu yoga honors the needs of the body. So let's start in easy pose," I say, fixing my eyes on a dark stain (perhaps from a candle?) on the parquet floor. My movements shaky, I demonstrate the pose. Self-consciously chanting "ohm" in front of strangers (where are my Kripalu buddies?), my body wilts. I barely manage a feeble *ohm*.

Nobody joins in. "In a seated, cross-legged position, inhale as you lift your right arm. Place your other hand near your hip and arc to the left. Repeat on the other side. Now, coming on your hands and knees, arch your back like a cat and then dip your belly for dog. Great!" So far so good. My voice gains momentum. The power of yoga takes over. I close the class with Sojo Henjo's ninth-century Zen poem that sees beauty where one least expects it:

> How mysterious!
> The lotus remains unstained
> By its muddy roots,
> Delivering shimmering
> Bright jewels from common dew.

"Thank you, Ann. See you next week." Their smiles and parting words reassure me that how I taught worked. Amazed I got through it without embarrassing myself, my heart is still beating fast when Peter peeks his head in the door. "Congratulations.

I overheard them praising your class. Glad to have you on the staff. Great start!"

Over time, I learn why my students are committed to yoga. A slender woman in her seventies with lively eyes and thick black hair with streaks of white always places her mat under the window. Her movements rigid and unstable, Beth explains, "I'm recovering from a stroke. Peter developed a strengthening regimen for me. Yoga is part of it." Her breathing is often labored, her face scrunched as if she bit into a sour lemon when pain catches her by surprise, but she never gives up. Over the next few months, her movements become less strained and her face looks more relaxed.

And then one day, Beth does not show up for class. She is absent the next class, and the one after that. Two months later, she returns pale and emaciated. She is wearing a red and white kerchief. "I had surgery for a breast tumor. I'm on chemo, and certain arm movements are painful. But I'm here!" Triumphantly, she rolls out her mat in her usual spot.

We all tell her we're sorry to hear what she's been through and how much we missed her. "Just do what feels comfortable," I say.

She never misses class. In the next few months, her hair grows back thicker and curlier than before. She isn't as pale, and her movements are stronger and more confident. Knowing I teach literature, Beth shares her excitement. "Our reading group is discussing Jonathan Franzen's novel *The Corrections*. What a good read! Didn't you tell me your students loved it?"

"Yes, and I loved teaching it. Wish you could have joined our discussions!"

"Last weekend, we picked apples at Ralph's Orchard. I taught my twin granddaughters how to make apple pie. Those girls sure keep me going!"

Not a word about her illness, treatments, or the pain she deals with. Though I taught her yoga, more valuable is what I learned from her—how to live like a fearless warrior.

One day, Jim, a dark-haired, stocky man in his late fifties, drops in to try out a yoga class. He makes distracting comments throughout the class to cover up his struggle with the postures. He knows muscle power and sweat but nothing about inner stillness and self-observation. Weeks pass, and his behavior begins to alienate the regulars. Just as I am getting up my courage to talk to him about it, something in his attitude changes.

No more rude remarks, no more clowning around. I catch him with eyes wide open stretching his chest and lengthening his spine in warrior II as if performing a magnificent musical symphony. Then students begin to greet him with a respectful nod when he sets up his mat behind Beth. When I hear his strong masculine voice chant "ohm," I know he has become part of our yogi family.

On a cold winter evening, I find Jim crouching on the floor waiting for the Pilates class to clear out of our room. With his shoulders slumped and head lowered toward the floor, he looks like an abandoned child.

"How are things going?" I ask while sliding down to the floor.

"Today was a really bad day. My divorce went through."

"Jim," I say in a low voice, "how are you managing? It must be so hard."

"I live in a small, dingy room downtown. I hate it." Tears well in his eyes, and his breathing is noisy. "Our family broke up. Kids, wife, house, a twenty-year marriage, everything gone," he says in a flat voice interspersed with deep sighs.

Silence is my best support. His vulnerability is palpable. I would like to give him a hug; instead, I whisper as we enter the aerobics room, "I hope yoga will make you feel better."

Looking straight at me, he nods. "It always does."

We never talk about his personal life again, but I can see he is gaining control over what is crushing his spirit when he is in his warriors, cobras, trees, and triangles. At least for the duration of the class, yoga is pulling him out of his sadness and pain.

Sarah, a school administrator in her mid-sixties, never makes it to class on time. She always sends an apologetic look as she hurriedly sets up her mat. Her face is drawn, her movements uncoordinated. Then one day, she shows up on time and in a state of disbelief announces, "I just retired!" She embarks on a regimen of canoeing, hiking, reading, and pursuing a disciplined yoga practice. In a few months, a new Sarah emerges: the deep lines of exhaustion gone from her face, body a few pounds lighter, eyes exuding a renewed vigor and calm. Overflowing with excitement, she explains, "How wonderful to do yoga without thinking about what's going on at work. It's just yoga and me!"

Sandra, a woman in her early forties, walks into class with her shoulders pulled toward her chest, face haggard, eyes downcast. Aloof and uncommunicative, she attends class sporadically. One day, she approaches me after class and asks, "Ann, could you please write down the Rumi quotation you read in our centering?"

"You mean 'Let the beauty we love be what we do'?"

"Yes, the lines hold a special meaning for me." And with no further explanation, she heads for the door. A few classes later, Sandra is ready to talk. She tells me a friend recommended she try yoga to deal with the recent loss of her husband. I flash to Margo's face when she suggested I try yoga for what was ailing me. With a grateful look, Sandra continues, "Yoga brings me momentary relief. My kids are small, and I had to go back to work. Things are really tough." And she swiftly makes her way to the door without giving me a chance to respond.

On my drive home, I cannot get Sandra's sad but grateful eyes out of my mind. I am deeply touched and humbled when I recall the caseful movements and relaxed faces of my students signaling that yoga's power is reaching them. My students faithfully show up for their weekly dose of healing yoga, the same way I did when I was a student in Antonio's and Carmen's classes. Now I am the one to pass on to others what I have received from my own yoga teachers.

One winter evening, it's dark when I arrive at the fitness center.

"Ann, you're welcome to have the candles I used in my Pilates class," Peter suggests when I step into the room.

Happy to avoid the harsh florescent lights, I distribute the red glass cups with candles around the floor as Peter gallantly lights them. The golden glow of the candles offsets the reflection of the traffic lights on the wall. The class begins, and the subtle movements of our bodies blend with the sound of flute music while the soft candlelight chases away uninvited thoughts. Concentrated energy pulls us together. I am transported to the Shadowbrook Room, where the flickering candles in Shiva's four hands dispel the surrounding darkness. The spirit of Kripalu has mysteriously shown up in our aerobics room in Upstate New York.

After teaching here for two and a half years, I must break the news. "In a few weeks, my husband and I are retiring to Maine. I'll miss you all and our class, but it's time for us to move on." Remembering my first class, I add, "You helped me ease into my role of a yoga teacher. I will be lucky to find such dedicated yogis in Brunswick."

On my last teaching day, there are a few packages and cards at the top of my yoga mat. Sarah explains the two framed photographs of a sunrise and sunset over the Vermont Mountains and Lake Champlain were taken from her porch. "You told us the Sanskrit word *hatha* merges two opposites: *ha* for 'sun' and *tha* for 'moon.' May that wholeness I found in this yoga class be with you on your journey."

Today, Sarah's photographs are still on the bookshelf in my Brunswick yoga room. Before she slips out of the room, Sandra places a book of Mary Oliver's poetry by my mat with a note: "Thank you for bringing me the beauty of yoga, and poetry, to remind me there is more to life than loss and despair, Sandra."

Teaching at the fitness center, I learned that human connections are more important than the settings we teach in. I used to dread driving into the bedlam of Consumer Square Plaza. But once on my mat, I retreated into the world of yoga. When merging our voices to chant "ohm," we became a cohesive yoga family, a near-miraculous advance over the first class when I chanted by myself. The people in the cars under our window would never suspect that we found in Consumer Square Plaza something that touches our souls, for which there is no price tag.

27: Helen's Story

A slender young woman walks into my English composition class in tight hip-hugger pants and a wide belt that accentuates the contours of her body. She is ten minutes late. Her big brown eyes take stock of the classroom. "Sooo, this is where I have to spend the *whole* semester? Well, here I am." Like a Hollywood celebrity, she walks toward the back of the room, nodding to friends and swaying her hips. Another semester of English 101 is on its way.

From her essays, I learn Helen is enthusiastic about sunsets, the late-night moon, the beauty of nature, and the pulse of life. She can be daring, serious, funny, and impulsive. She likes to read and discuss life-probing questions. She loves to write. She participates in class discussions only when she is interested in the topic, but mostly, she is tuned out with a vacant gaze.

The next semester, Helen's name is on the roster for my Philosophy and Practice of Yoga honors seminar. This course is structured around yoga philosophy readings, a rigorous yoga practice, journal writing, and four papers. Helen practices yoga with a wide grin as if she has won an unexpected prize: her movements are focused, her attitude serious, and her papers express a deep feeling for yoga. Not until the next semester, when she registers for my Autobiographical Writing class, do I learn why yoga is so important to her.

Her story comes in installments. The semester she was taking English 101, she was in a marijuana and alcohol haze. She failed the breath test when caught for erratic driving and was sent to a drug rehabilitation program. This left her angry at the police, the drug counselors, her divorced parents, and the world in general. Defiant, she continued to do drugs and drink and to cheat on her urine tests.

Her quivering voice trails off as she finishes reading her draft. Her face beet-red, she lowers her eyes toward the floor. Nineteen sets of glossy eyes are glued to her lowered head. Extemporaneously, a chain of vigorous applause thunders through the room. Guardedly, Helen lifts her face. A few students walk over to hug her. It is clear Helen mastered the most powerful writing tool: having the courage to tell the unadorned truth.

Later, we listen to Helen's description of an encounter session at the drug rehabilitation center. Here, she met older drug addicts with ruined lives and health who were unable to hold onto jobs or promises. Did she want to end up like this? Instead of blaming the authorities for classifying her as a drug addict, she started to see her future, and herself, in a different light.

In a few weeks, we get the rest of the story. Something shifted in her thinking. She realized she wasn't a great hero esteemed by her drug-using friends. She discovered something needed to change—not with the cop, her mother and father, or the drug rehab counselors, but with her, Helen. She stopped sneaking around with friends who did drugs and drank. She stopped cheating on her urine tests. She stopped lying to others and to herself. Her rebellious stance lost its power once she dropped out of the circle of drug users and mended her family relationships. The transition from one lifestyle to another was lonely. My Philosophy and Practice of Yoga course coincided with her first baby steps into that new drug-free life. This is how Helen explained her love for yoga in her final exam:

Before yoga, it was impossible for me to listen to my body. It was impossible to sit in silence without my mind racing a mile a minute with so many thoughts clouding my judgment at every step....Yoga has allowed me to become sensitive to every little detail of the day that brings joy....Yoga encourages change, acceptance, and constant self-improvement.

Why be stuck with such a past when there is no time machine to go back and change it all... By not needing or depending on anything but myself, I am able to trust my soul and utilize all the advantages I can bring to myself and anyone else.... But I must know myself before I can trust myself. Yoga is a great tool for learning about the Self. It clears the mind of all the turmoil and allows you to truly listen to inner thoughts and feelings.

In her description of how she transitioned from chaos to clarity and destructive behaviors to more constructive ones, Helen captures, with remarkable insight, what I went through on my own transformative journey. Like a bee who drinks nectar from a flower for its sustenance, Helen clung to yoga for support.

The supportive class response helped her regain her lost pride. She admitted to her classmates and to me that she had messed up her life but was fixing it up. After she finished reading her last installment, her fellow classmates admitted to destructive behaviors they wished they were strong enough to break: having one-night stands, struggling with diet, smoking, avoiding responsibility for poor study habits, and sabotaging relationships. All of a sudden, Helen had become, in their eyes, a heroic model of someone who had faced her own failings and overcome them.

It was quite a journey for her, the class, and for me.

This is how she describes it in her final:

I have learned more useful information in this class than in my entire four semesters at college, my entire high school career and in anything I have ever done in my life. You should know that yoga excites me, and I would like to bring the practice and philosophy to as many people as possible. If only they could experience the satisfaction life can bring when you push aside all the complications the mind brings on and breathe deeply into the bottom of your belly and focus on the stillness that is within us all.

Those moments where the hair rises on my arms, or the feeling of endorphins releasing in my brain were like distant feelings of happiness I couldn't quite connect with at first.... Having never allowed myself to truly absorb a moment of bliss where my spirit bursts through my skin with joy...that unattainable feeling of happiness was reached the first day of yoga class and every day afterwards.

28: Intimacy with Strangers

Young ballet dancers in Brunswick, Maine; a high-school girls'
soccer team in Popham Beach, Maine; a family on a remote
farm in Bortne, Poland; middle-aged women seeking solace in
Plattsburgh, New York. The one common thread is the opportunity of experiencing yoga in unusual places at unexpected
times. I may never see these people again, although through
yoga, a momentary closeness transpired that will stay with me
ever after.

Less than a year after I become certified to teach yoga, I
happen to share my enthusiasm for its ability to both relax and
restore one's positive energies with a casual acquaintance who
teaches at a ballet studio. The conversation results in an offer
to teach a yoga class to her ballet students. This is how Terry
explains what they want: "Our ballet students must learn to
relax. A once-a-week yoga class would be a perfect antidote to
what we exact from them in our structured routines."

A group of slender girls sporting leotards, ballet shoes, and
pulled-back hairstyles turn their heads in my direction when I
walk into the dance studio. The mirror-lined walls with wood-
en hand bars and the cracks in the linoleum attest to the long

hours these aspiring ballerinas put into their ballet routines. I am carrying a yoga mat under my arm, a colorful bag with a chime, homemade straps and eye bags, a tote bag hoisted on my shoulder with a book of Danna Fauld's poetry, a typed-out posture sequence, and a CD called *Stillness* that features gentle piano music. In my free hand, I am carrying a portable CD player.

These students, aged thirteen to seventeen, are well-versed in the discipline of structured movement but have had no experience with the mind/body interaction of a yoga class. I am here to get them to stretch, flex, rotate, twist, and most importantly, to enjoy a different form of movement. Their undisguised curiosity energizes me.

Though they giggle when I tell them we do yoga in bare feet, they wiggle their toes in the newfound freedom after they pull off their ballet stockings. We start with a centering. "Come into a cross-legged seated pose," I instruct. "Close your eyes. What are you feeling right now? Observe without judgment."

After a few rounds of yogic breathing, their nervous energy fades like a transition between scenes in a movie. Well-trained to follow instructions, they move into the postures with striking elegance. With legs and arms extending to the far reaches of their mats, they make stunning warriors, steady trees, and swanlike cobras. Time slips by quickly.

It is getting dark outside when I instruct in a hushed voice, "In preparation for deep relaxation, stretch out on your spine. Let go of any willful holding. Imagine you are drifting down a quiet river lined with willow trees swaying in the wind." I turn off the florescent lights. Darkness covers their bodies like a cozy blanket. Nineteen motionless bodies with rice-filled eye bags covering their eyes slip into stillness. The soft piano music offsets the sound of their teachers' conversations in the hallway. After a few minutes, I tap my chime to bring deep relaxation to a close.

Nobody moves. The streetlamp shining through the window sheds a dim light on their silhouettes, but the expressions on their faces remain hidden. *What are they thinking? What are they feeling?* Aware their teachers are impatiently waiting to resume the scheduled ballet class, I get them into a seated position for a final centering. I conclude with a short poem about yoga's ability to connect us with ourselves. Neither a sound nor movement disturbs the warm quiet. Yoga's sensory language is doing its silent talking.

As if coming from far away, one girl's spontaneous clapping breaks the silence. Within seconds, the rest of the class joins in a roaring outburst. Not a word is spoken. Overcome with emotion, I gather my things and tiptoe quietly into the lit hallway. The harsh lights assault my eyes. I overhear the impatient voice of their instructor telling them to position themselves at their bars as I push the door to leave the building. The sound of spontaneous clapping is still resounding in my ears when I turn the ignition key. I never expected that after this very first yoga class, these young dancers would respond to yoga's alluring power with such jubilant gratitude.

The morning's fresh ocean air is the perfect introduction to the day. The path to Popham Beach is lined with wild rose bushes in full bloom, which perfume the air with their sweet scent. Determined, Dennis and I drag our seaside equipment through the sandy path. Finally, the payoff: sparkling water views from left to right and endless stretches of white sand in front of us. The sight of crashing waves quickens our pace as the ocean smells grow stronger. Down by the water, the packed wet sand massages my bare feet. Admiring their extensive wingspan, I wave to the energetic gulls gliding through the air.

Twenty-two schoolgirls in team shorts and T-shirts huddle in front of us; otherwise, the beach is deserted. The comforting sound of clamoring waves caressing the edge of the beach reminds me of the subtle presence of incoming and outgoing breaths during a yoga practice. Luminescent sunlight sparkles across the water the way the sun salutation flow radiates through me when I move through its twelve interwoven postures.

"It would be great to do yoga in this incredible setting!" I say flippantly.

Before Dennis has a chance to answer, a girl with a cute ponytail and broad smile asks, "Do you know how to do yoga?"

"Yes. I'm a yoga teacher."

"Hey, would you do some yoga with us?" calls out a girl who is kicking a soccer ball around.

"Sure. It's a wild idea, but why not?" I immediately start planning out a routine that will work in the sinking sand. Shy Dennis gets as far away as he can and immediately buries his face in his book.

Brushing the sand off their legs and facing the waves, the girls form three long lines. "Let's drink in this wonderful air," I tell them. "Take a deep breath through the nose, mouth closed. With an inhale, lift your arms overhead. Lower them as you bend forward on an exhale." The girls follow my commands, eyes aglow, faces concentrated. Like a conductor, I bring their individual movements into orchestral unity. The cool ocean breeze is blowing our hair, and the wet sand, silky to the touch, is massaging our feet.

A swift reach of their arms overhead excites a chorus of screeching gulls circling above our heads. "Look at the sun's golden reflection on the gulls' white bellies!" I weave this image into my verbal cues. Twenty-two heads turn toward the sky. "And now transition into a forward bend, touching the damp sand with your fingertips." A colony of gulls goes into a frenzy of glides and dips as we lower our spines toward the sand. Their screeches override my instructional narrative.

"Dig your feet into the sand, lunge forward with your right leg, and lift your arms shoulder height for warrior II." Energized by the sight of twenty-two moving bodies in a dance-like flow, I turn their attention to their sensations. "What are you feeling right now? Empowered? Grounded? Strong?" These teens, no longer girls yet not quite women, explore their warrior power with smiles and glowing eyes. Their soccer coach arrives and watches from a distance as his team turns into trees, dancers, warriors, and eagles. With their hair flying, legs firmly anchored in the sand, arms swinging in the air, and faces glowing in the golden sunlight, they look like goddesses.

Impatient to start the soccer game, the coach calls out, "Girls, time to hustle. Finish the yoga and separate into two groups." He gives me a friendly wave to acknowledge he enjoyed our performance.

"You guys are terrific! What powerful warriors!" I praise them with genuine admiration.

"We loved it. Yoga is great! Thank you! Thank you! Thank you!" they call after me as I trudge through the sand to rejoin Dennis.

Flushed and revved up, I settle under the umbrella. "That was quite a performance!" Dennis says, looking up from his book. "You sure stirred the gulls up. And the girls were awesome!"

I pull out my book and bury my feet in the warm, powdery sand. I can identify the words on the page, but I can't make out their meaning. Instead of reading someone else's story, my own emerges.

My memory carries me to Cape Breton Island, which we visited two summers ago. With my legs buried in the sand, eyes following the gliding gulls, hair ruffled in the ocean breeze, I am stretching into the expanse of a warrior, at one with the ocean, sky, gulls, and sun. My mind returns to the immediate past when twenty-two soccer players merged with nature's intoxicating life force. I think of the ancient yogis, who practiced outdoors in the early morning hours to be part of nature's awakening energy, and how powerful it was to experience that same feeling this morning.

By the time the girls' game is over, the beach is filled with sun-worshipping crowds and squealing children splashing in the water. The early morning magic is gone. Now it is just an ordinary beach day, the smell of sunscreen wafting through the air and gulls tugging at people's bags in search of sandwiches and chips. It is hard to believe that only a few hours ago, we had a magical yoga practice on this very same beach. Like a fleeting emotion, an unannounced sensation, or a passing breath, that practice is by now nothing but an unforgettable memory.

We stay on the Horbal family farm with two daughters, a son, two dogs, and seven cows when we visit the birthplace of my husband's grandfather in remote Bortne in Poland's Carpathian Mountains. Andrej and Dennis are distant cousins. There is always a pot of soup simmering on the wood-burning stove, mushrooms drying above the stove, and a pot of milk forming a thick layer of cream to make butter and cheese on the side of the stove. Kristyna, always cheerful and energetic, cooks, bakes, and takes care of the children and farm chores from early morning until late at night. When I tell her, in a mixture of Czech, Russian, and her local dialect Lemko, that in the early morning, I open the balcony door to practice yoga in view of Jamora Mountain, she asks, "What's yoga?"

"It will be easier if I show you this evening," I reply.

After the cows are milked, dishes done, and children in bed, I demonstrate a few yoga postures along with basic yogic breathing. A quick learner, she is thrilled with the results. "Wow, my spine feels so much better. Do you think yoga would help Natalka with her scoliosis?"

"Why don't we try it on Sunday?" I say, excited at the prospect of doing yoga with her shy daughter, who reads curled up on the porch when not helping with house chores.

When back from church, Kristyna and Natalka run upstairs to put their gym outfits on while Dennis and I push the dining room furniture aside and roll out thick woolen blankets as makeshift yoga mats.

The curious widowed grandfather, his buddy from next door, nine-year-old Jaroslav, and Kristyna's husband Andrej settle on the dining room chairs we reset against the wall. They watch our every move as if we are doing the yoga for their entertainment. A first for me, I teach in a foreign language with more onlookers than practitioners.

Four-year-old Irinka sits at the edge of her mother's blanket amused at her warrior followed by a cobra. In an attempt to imitate her movements, she collapses on the floor in a fit of laughter. Eleven-year-old Natalka concentrates on her movements despite the presence of the inquisitive audience. When the aroma of cooked chicken seeps into the room, it signals that it is time to bring the yoga class to a close. Without delay, I get them into the corpse pose for deep relaxation.

Little Irinka puts her head close to her mother's face and shakes her corpse-like body with all her might. When nothing happens, she cries out in a pitiful voice, "Dear Mother, please, please come back to me, come back."

Her lower lip quivers, her eyes water. Grabbing her mother's arms, she shakes her once more time, her voice frantic. "Mommy, Mommy, get up, get up." No longer able to suppress her laughter, Kristyna throws her arms around Irinka, who hugs her mother in a tight embrace. Irinka's crisis is over, or is it?

"Please, dear Mommy," Irinka pleads before she puts a spoonful of homemade noodles in her mouth. "Don't ever do yoga again. I don't like the way you die when you do it."

Kristyna smiles reassuringly. "Can't you see I'm back just the way I always am?" She plants a big kiss on Irinka's cheek.

And so this is, to Irinka's great delight, the one and only yoga class in the history of Bortne, a village with two hundred inhabitants high up in the Carpathian Mountains, where they had never heard of yoga before I got there.

"Is this Ann? I'm calling about yoga," an unfamiliar woman's voice explains. "I'm looking for someone to give me private lessons. I saw the flyer about your yoga classes on the library bulletin board. Would you be interested in giving me a private class?"

Why not? I think. We settle on a price, day, and time.

The streets are snow-covered when I slip out of the house to meet my first private student. Except for the sound of crunching snow under my boots, it is a quiet Saturday morning. A shy but kind-looking middle-aged woman in workout clothes opens the door. I scan the framed photographs of weddings, grown children, and grandchildren wondering if she is divorced or widowed. I ask no questions. She gives no explanations.

She places her mat between the couch and the glass door that faces the snow-covered backyard, which sparkles like diamonds in the bright January sun. I squeeze my mat alongside the couch, ready to start the class. "How long have you been doing yoga? Do you have any health issues I should know about?"

"Not very long. I have a cranky knee, but I'll manage what I can."

"Let's start with a centering. Take a yogic breath from the depths of your belly. Scan your body to see what you're feeling in your hips, knees, and spine." Watching her closely, I adjust my cues to match her hesitant movements. When the strained expression leaves her face, I hold the postures a bit longer so she can synchronize her movements with mine. She watches my every move as if I am leading her to an undisclosed destination, the way I watched Carmen in my pre-Kripalu days. "Bend your right knee ninety degrees, bring your arms up shoulder height, focus your gaze. Yes, that's it. What a beautiful warrior I. What are you feeling right now?"

The posture practice complete, I guide her through a full body scan to bring her into a satisfying deep relaxation. "Let go of willful holding. If a thought comes, let it drift away like a cloud. Surrender to your inner silence." Knowing my teaching is done, my body relaxes. I look at the tree's long shadow on the snow to settle the emotions the practice stirred in me.

Once we're back in easy pose, I notice her shoulders are swaying forward and back in ever faster circular movements. Uncontrollable cries that become deep sobs shake her body as if wild winds are sweeping through her. Silent, I wait for this unforeseen outburst to subside. Still sniffling, she says with a surprised look on her face, "I have no idea what happened. I never cry."

"It's not uncommon for a yoga practice to release stored-up tension," I reply in a calm voice. I think back to the early stages of my own practice when uncontrollable tears rolled down my cheeks during deep relaxation. "You'll be surprised to find that one day, instead of tears, there will be a peaceful calm. That's what happened to me," I say.

When parting, she asks, "Will you be free to come next week?"

To witness how yoga unlocks built-up tension in response to my teaching is awe-inspiring. Two strangers who know nothing about each other's lives share an unexpected moment of intimacy. When I was a student of yoga, my teachers made me aware of yoga's power to do this. Now, as a yoga teacher, I am the one who dissipates the sadness in others.

I take a long walk to give the upsurge of emotion time to settle before I go home. I think of the day I received my red Pioneer scarf, which made me feel I had something special to offer the collective that accepted me as one of them. Today, I am feeling what it is like to offer that something special to another human being seeking a deeper connection to herself.

29: *Yogaville*

A 2003 cover from *The New Yorker* magazine has a woman in a mediation pose with curled wiry fingers on her knees, shoulders scrunched, and lips pulled back as if she's on the verge of a scream. Her narrowed eyes follow a fly buzzing around her head. Though I laugh, it makes me think about the harmful effect of stress on one's body. With two years of yoga teaching behind me, I am aware of my students' struggles with headaches, high blood pressure, depression, fatigue, and sleeping disorders. Is there something in addition to yoga that would help alleviate this stress? A search on the Internet reveals a two-week stress management training for yoga teachers at the monastic yoga community at Virginia's Yogaville ashram. *Wouldn't this training make me a more effective yoga teacher?* My sights are set. A prerequisite for acceptance into the program is an established meditation practice, which I don't have but now must begin. Where do I start?

Jack Kornfield! His book, *Meditation for Beginners: Six Guided Meditations for Insight, Inner Clarity, and Cultivating a Compassionate Heart*, is my guide into the world of stillness. Despite the easy-to-follow cues he delivers in a hushed voice on the CD that came with the book, I am a meditation disaster: my right foot falls asleep, my nose itches, and each time I lose the connection to my breath, the incessant chatter in my head takes over. Kornfield never tires of reminding me that focusing on my breath is certain to pull me away from my distracting mind. Obligated to be a meditator by the fast-approaching date for the stress management training, I sit obediently on my couch cushion every morning. I fluctuate between tolerable and unbearable restlessness. My struggle to stay connected to my breath is far from over the day I board the plane for Yogaville.

At the Charlottesville airport, a middle-aged man in shorts and a T-shirt is holding up a sign with "Yogaville" in big black letters. "Hi, I'm Derek. We'll be at Yogaville in about an hour," he explains as he leads our small group of arrivals to a parked van. He patiently answers our questions about life at Yogaville as we drive through rolling hills and lush forests and fields. We learn that Derek is a psychologist on a year's retreat at the ashram. "We've arrived!" he announces when he drives up to some modest buildings behind a thick row of tall trees.

It is early afternoon, and the Virginia sun in June is keeping everybody inside. "It's so magical and peaceful here, I feel I've landed in Shangri-la," I say as I follow Derek to a three-story building at the end of the quad.

"Here's your dorm. Your welcome packet with your schedule is in your room." These are his last words before he takes off.

My spartan room on the third floor has four bunk beds with a view of the empty quad. I drop my belongings on a bottom bunk and run out to explore the grounds. White and yellow chamomiles, hot pink mountain laurels, and bright yellow and coral lilies line the path above the fast-moving waters of the James River. Their sensual fragrance slows my pace.

Charmed by the lush scenery, I follow the path like an explorer on a deserted planet where time has stopped. The silence is punctuated by fast-moving water splashing over big boulders. Like a princess in nature's palace, I am entertained by the hum of bugs and bees fluttering from flower to flower and the high-pitched sounds of colorful birds. I welcome this soothing solitude like a thirsty pilgrim.

By the time I get back to my dorm, my roommate Sharon, a petite woman in her forties with thick black hair and a pleasant soft-spoken manner, is neatly arranging her clothes on the shelves behind the bed across from mine.

"I did my teacher training here. Where did you get your certification?" she asks.

"I trained at Kripalu. By the way, who was this Swami Satchidananda?"

"A much-beloved guru, he founded this place in 1980. He was big on yoga and health. He, as they say here, passed out of his body two years ago. Every day, they read from his writings during our silent lunches."

"Where do the swamis live?"

"The eighteen swamis live in a building outsiders never get to see. It's somewhere over there." She walks over to the window to show me a thick forest behind the quad.

"I know nothing about ashram life, swamis, and gurus..."

"You'll quickly get to know how special this place is," she says as we make our way to the dining room building.

After dinner, I meet my nine classmates and two instructors, Swami Vidyananda, a lively, intelligent, articulate woman in her fifties with a delightful sense of humor, and Swami Ramananda, whose kind, contemplative manner immediately puts me at ease. Relieved our manual is not as thick as the one I had to work through at Kripalu, I take detailed notes on stress and how it manifests in our bodies. By 9:00 p.m., we are sent to rest up for the 6:00 a.m. meditation.

At 5:00 a.m., I awake to enchanting violin music. I jump out of bed and look down the hallway, where I see a tall figure clothed in a flowing orange robe, which is worn by all the swamis as a symbol of fire and sun. She has a bun of white hair and gently sways her head to the soft movements of her violin bow. At the end of the hall, she vanishes like a mirage. Her music lingers in the air like a fragrant perfume. I learn that the mirage is Swami Gurucharanda or "Mataji" who, every morning, wakes us in time for meditation with the elevating sounds of her violin virtuosity.

Meditation, the bedrock of this community's life, is built into our daily routine. Swamis meditate three times a day, before breakfast, lunch, and dinner. Our class meditates one hour before breakfast in the Academy Building and a half hour at noon in the pink-domed temple with sky-blue overtones, which is shaped like a multi-petaled lotus. Here, unlike the world I come from, meditation is as normal as breathing or brushing your teeth.

"Meditation is like a little puppy dog," Shilmurti, an Indian woman on the teaching staff, tells me with a disarming smile that lights up the delicate features of her face. "All day long, this playful puppy demands attention from its master. When visitors arrive, the puppy, unhappy to be ignored, misbehaves."

"I don't get it. What does this have to do with meditation?"

"That puppy is like your mind. It needs to be trained to quiet its relentless demand for your attention," Shilmurti says, pleased to see how surprised I am.

"So, meditation is a form of mind training? Sort of like dog training?"

"You can think of it that way."

Shilmurti suggests I use *ohm* as a mantra instead of my breath if it does not disturb my inner calm. In search of a personalized mantra, I experiment with Czech words. I start with *mír* (peace), but it does not feel quite right. I switch to *láska* (love), but too many emotions interfere. I try *slunce* (sun) followed by *slunečnice* (sunflower). My heart beats faster and my breath quickens when I repeat these seemingly innocent words. I decide there will be no Czech, English, or Sanskrit mantra. After that, I meditate exclusively on my breath to bypass the emotional reaction language evokes in me.

Early the next morning, I am trying to chase away my worries about my upcoming teaching test while I squirm restlessly on my meditation cushion. *Will I be effective? Will my nervousness make me forget something important?* My hips are uncomfortable, my shoulders are heavy, and my right knee is complaining. I am hungry and fed up with my inability to surrender to meditation's tranquility. *Return to your breath and stop thinking or you'll never get through a whole hour in this aggravated state,* I reprimand myself.

The sound of chirping birds shifts my attention to the wide range of sounds that resemble individual instruments in an orchestra: high, low, shrill, long, short, pleasant, and weird. My breath calms to support me in finding relief from my distracted state. Slipping into a soothing oblivion, I forget about my squeaky hip, my moody knee, and my stiff spine. As if enfolded in a soft, puffy feather quilt, I have no desire to move or think. I surrender to this unexpected retreat from my controlling mind with a mind and body at peace.

Beaming from ear to ear, I run up to Shilmurti to report what happened. "Today's meditation felt like I grew an umbilical cord to my inner stillness. It nourished and strengthened my spirit. The weight lifted off my shoulders, the tightness in my jaw released, and my limbs loosened. The periods of silence got longer and longer. It was like I was being carried away on a cloud."

Squeezing me in a tight hug, she asks in her charming Indian accent, "Ann, now do you believe in meditation's magical power?"

Propped up on a pile of blue cushions, I work methodically on my final take-home exam in an empty practice room in the basement of our dorm. In five pages of neat handwriting, I show my instructors everything I know about managing stress. It is late. Bleary-eyed, I drag myself up the three flights to my room feeling good about how much I learned during these two weeks. Sharon signals with one finger on her lips, without letting up the rapid movement of her other hand, to keep quiet. She looks overwhelmed. I give her a sympathetic look before I collapse on my bed. In a few hours, the violin will be calling me to my meditation cushion. I get my exam back with thoughtful comments that confirm I am certified to teach stress management.

It is time to get down to the Lotus Temple for my last noontime meditation. Desperate for fresh air, I decide to walk through the forest instead of riding in the van with the rest of the students. I am distracted by a crackling sound on the path ahead of me. I spot a figure in an orange robe moving through the trees at a fast clip. I recognize Swami Ramananda, who slows down when he hears my footsteps. We ease into a pleasant conversation. He is curious about my relationship to yoga. I am curious about his life in New York City at the Integral School of Yoga. After I describe how yoga has changed my life, Swami Ramananda asks how my husband is reacting to those changes.

For the first time, I stop to think about what it is like for my husband, a practicing Orthodox, to watch my deepening involvement with yoga and now meditation. Is his prayer comparable to my meditation? Is his religious faith as grounding as yoga is for me? I think of all the times I have accompanied him to his church services, not as a participant, but as an observing outsider. I love the soulful choir music, the artful icons, the meditative effect of lit beeswax candles, the scent of incense permeating the air, and the beauty of the bearded priests' robes. I can relate to the drama of what is going on but not its substance. "Yes," I say with a hint of surprise in my voice, "he's quite comfortable with my efforts to meditate. In some ways, it brings me closer to his world."

Swami Ramananda gives a name to my experience: a spiritual journey. Did I even have the vocabulary to define my search? How do I, a child brought up to believe in a Communist ideology that was man-made and not God-given, find a home for my wandering soul? As a novice meditator, I am still caught up in mastering the technique, but as someone who lives a contemplative life, Swami Ramananda imperceptibly shifts my attention to the deeper purpose of meditation and yoga.

Swami Ramananda slows down when he spots a large bush with ripe blackberries at the edge of the forest. He pushes the prickly branches aside, and with a boyish smile, he puts a few plump blackberries, still warm from the hot sun, into my hand. They are sweet and juicy. At this moment, he is more than a swami with an enigmatic spiritual life I am trying to comprehend; he is a fellow human being who loves nature—and life—as much as I do.

When we get out of the woods, we join the people rushing to get to the Lotus Temple before the noontime bell goes off. I pick up a coral-colored cushion and climb the narrow spiral staircase to the heart of the Lotus. I retain the glow of the lights behind my closed eyes for a few more seconds before I sink into my meditation. Swami Ramananda's wise words fade out before my mind switches off. Silence around me. Silence within me. The intoxication of stillness. Wordlessness. Mind dissolving in the body; body receptive to the mind's disposition. I am nourished and refueled. Meditation connects me to an inner world that belongs to me alone. In the depths of my being resides a self that cannot be harmed or hurt, an elusive part of my being I am in touch with whenever I meditate.

I seek out Swami Ramananda's calm face as soon as the chime brings our meditation to a close. His eyes are still closed when I send him a big smile of gratitude for being such a generous, caring spirit. He is a man at peace with himself and his mission in life. He already knows what I am still discovering—that yoga and meditation are opening me to explore new ways of managing my life. The sweet flavor of blackberries is still on my tongue when I lean forward to pick up my meditation cushion. I feel Dennis's presence as I make my way down the spiral staircase and into the bright sun shining on the colorful flowers lining the pathway to the temple.

On the eve of our departure, our instructors smile mystifyingly as they busy themselves with big basins of steaming water, jars of cream, and towels. When invited to enter our classroom, we find warm basins of aromatic water in front of our chairs.

"Please submerge your feet while the water is still warm," Swami Vidyananda prods us. Then she pulls my hair back, fastening it with hairpins. With gentle strokes, she applies a smooth white cream to my face. As the cream dries, it tightens the skin around my lips.

Swami Vidyananda interrupts our giggling with an un-expected question. "What do you do to care for yourselves?"

"I soak in the bath, but I don't take time for a facial or a leisurely soak with scented essential oil," I admit, stroking the silky feel of my cheeks.

"A little pampering and self-care are as important as yoga, meditation, or a walk in nature. How you treat yourself affects how you think and act, and that affects how you feel." Swami Vidyananda urges us not to take the importance of self-care lightly.

"Okay, once a week I'm going to soak my feet. My feet feel like new!" Sharon says with a girlish chuckle.

Swami Vidyananda cautions us, "Don't let old habits creep back when you get home. Remember, we want to reduce, not induce, stress."

I take a break from packing for my next day's departure to read to Sharon from notes I took during Swami Ramananda's closing lecture about muscular memory earlier that morning: "A balanced mind can't be found in an unbalanced body. Pos-tures are part of yoga but are not its aim. The aim is balance.... We gain mastery of our bodies and minds if, with acceptance, we listen rather than impose on them. Muscular memory means everything we do with the mind affects the body." I look up from my notes. "If memories are retained in the body's muscular memory, what happens to what we don't want to re-member?" I ask Sharon, who looks distressed.

She confesses, "I'm not ready to face what's waiting for me at home." She swallows and blinks, her eyes tearing. "My husband and I barely speak. We're both afraid to admit our relationship is destroying us. While here, I didn't have a single migraine. Isn't my body telling me something?"

Waving my notebook in the air, I say, "Remember, we can fool the head but not the body. Isn't that what we've learned? Let's see how we'll manage our stress when we go back to the real world."

Snapping her suitcase shut, Sharon says resolutely, "Yes, it's time to bring the textbook wisdom into my own life."

30: Facing the Real World

A loud announcement at the Charlottesville airport interrupts my reading in *Will Yoga & Meditation Really Change My Life?* edited by Stephen Cope. "We regret to announce the flight to Pittsburgh is cancelled due to technical difficulties. Please come to the ticket agent to rebook your flights." I can't believe the coincidence between what is happening and the skit we acted out in the stress management class two days ago.

My group was tasked with the following scenario: You are at the airport with your family and your flight is cancelled until the next day. React as stressfully as you can. Be melodramatic. As the oldest student in the class, I am the designated "mother," and Swami Ramananda is my "husband." Our two "bratty children" and an "overwhelmed airline representative" complete the cast. Swami Ramananda, although trying hard to act upset, is no match to my shrill voice and wild hand movements. After dumping our frustration on the overwhelmed airline representative, our dysfunctional family disintegrates into hysteria. As soon as we resort to the first rule for managing stress—STOP—our shrieking and emoting come to a standstill.

After a few rounds of deep breaths, my "husband" and I reassess our options. With our voices a few decibels lower and breathing more even, our thinking is clearer. Though our situation has not changed, our attitudes have.

I suggest, "Let's have some fun!"

"How about spending the night in a hotel?" my "husband" replies.

Jumping up and down, the "kids" chime in. "We can play games and order pizza! Yay!" After which we return to our seats to the applause of our amused classmates.

This was a staged drama with a predictable outcome. Now I am about to find out what is going to happen in the real-life drama at the Charlottesville airport.

At the sight of the tightly drawn faces and clenched teeth of my fellow travelers, I am itching to teach what I have learned: in a situation that can't be changed, the only thing you can control is your own behavior. Why not ride it out over a coffee or a beer, or get absorbed in a good book? Instead of pursuing that wild idea, I bury my head in my book until I board my plane for Pittsburgh, pleased with how calm and focused I have been.

Aimlessly, I stroll through the crowded walkways of the Pittsburgh airport with four hours to kill. I scan sandwiches filled with meat and cheese, rich pastries, ice cream, and slices of pizza with streaks of oil and circles of fatty sausage and pepperoni glistening under the heater lamps. My stomach shuts down at the thought of eating this kind of food after two weeks on a vegan diet. By accident, I stumble on a deserted section of the airport. My body is craving its daily dose of stretches. *Why not do some yoga right here?* Making sure I am alone, I take my shoes and jacket off, then lower myself to the carpeted floor.

When going into a lunge, I sense somebody is looking at me. A slightly overweight middle-aged woman in shorts and a loose blouse with an employee badge around her neck is walking laps between the aisles. When she gets closer, she asks, "What are you doing?"

"Yoga."

"Really? That looks interesting."

"Have you ever done yoga?"

"No, but I'd like to try it."

"Are you sure?"

"Yeah. I'm on my work break. I clean the planes between flights."

"How do you feel about taking your sneakers off?"

Switching to my measured teaching voice, I move us through a series of warm-ups. She lets out pleasurable sounds as she moves, and we progress to simple postures. With each stretch, the glow on her face deepens. In deep relaxation, she trustingly releases her body to the carpeted floor. When I bring her out of the relaxation, she looks dazed.

"I was in a happy place. This stuff is great!" She looks at me appreciatively.

"I'm so glad it worked for you."

"Have you been visiting someone?" she wants to know.

"I just spent two weeks at a yoga ashram getting my certification to teach stress management. It's about an hour outside of Charlottesville."

"Amazing. I never heard of a place like that." Pulling out a thick meat sandwich, she hands me half.

"It's kind of you to share your dinner," I say. "But after two weeks without meat, I'm not quite ready. Why don't you tell me something about yourself instead?"

I get her life story of a wasted youth spent addicted to drugs, a situation that changed when she found religion and a man she loves. With a loving expression, she describes how embracing the teachings of Jesus saved her life. "For the first time ever, I felt good about myself. I don't dwell on the past. I live for the happiness I have now." Her parting words: "I like yoga. I can't thank you enough."

"I will always remember our impromptu yoga class at the Pittsburgh airport," I call out as I leave for my boarding gate.

I board the plane high on life, high on yoga, high on what is awaiting me.

31: Bringing Yogaville to Plattsburgh

Bursting with energy, I return to my teaching responsibilities with this little secret warming my soul—if stressed, I know what to do about it. Colleagues and friends approach me with stories about their stress as if my training made me an overnight expert. This is what I never knew about them: Jeff has a stressful relationship with his mother, Sophie disapproves of her teen son's lifestyle, Carl is unhappy about not being promoted, and Amanda is torn between the needs of her aging parents and her growing family. Uncertain if they just want to talk or if they are seeking a remedy, I play the part of a willing listener—that is, until Nicole approaches me.

I know Nicole as a respected faculty member and an accomplished writer—a slender woman in her early forties always professionally dressed, with her brown hair neatly arranged around her intelligent face. When she catches up with me on the staircase of our office building, her face flushed, she asks in a harried voice, "I heard you're back from a stress management training program. Do you have a moment to talk?"

Curious about what is behind this sudden interest, I reply, "Sure. How about a cup of coffee?"

Her face lights up. "That would be great! Now?"

Seated at a corner table in the student union, we exchange a few minutes of casual chatter before Nicole gets to what is really bothering her. Biting her lower lip, she blurts out, "I'm tense, stressed out, overcommitted—I'm worn out! Is there some quick way of dealing with this?"

"Can you describe what exactly you're struggling with?" I ask.

Resting her chin in her hand, she explains, "In a word, *balance*. I'm stressed about what I want to accomplish and what I actually *do* accomplish. However hard I try, it's never good enough." Waving her hand as punctuation, she accidentally tips her coffee. After profuse apologies and while mopping up the spill with a napkin, she continues. "My parents prided themselves on perfectionism. I could never measure up to their standards. However much I accomplish, I still feel inadequate."

I have always thought of her as highly accomplished and successful. I am shocked to realize the discrepancy between her impeccable public image and her private life. I sip my tea, assessing the best approach.

"How do you feel about having a meditation practice? I could certainly help with that. It might be worth taking a closer look at what causes you stress before we develop an appropriate coping strategy."

She considers my words. "Are you sure this will work?"

"You'll only know if you try. I suggest you give a consistent practice a couple of weeks before you dismiss it completely. Managing stress includes deep yogic breathing, meditation, attitude adjustments, and of course, yoga."

Nicole looks skeptical. "Those are major lifestyle changes. I would never have time for that."

"Once you learn the basic techniques, the practice itself requires only short time segments. For now, let's start with naming a typical situation that causes you stress."

Her eyes reflect discomfort; her face and body stiffen. "I have so much stress! There's no relief."

Gently, I urge, "Describe just one stressor, step by step. It can be something insignificant."

Nicole hesitates. "I'm not used to talking about this."

"Nicole, I'm not here to judge, only to help. Truly, there's no right or wrong in this game. Give just one simple example, if you can."

"Okay. Here's something really silly. Yesterday, displeased with how I made the bed, I redid it several times. The sheets still weren't smooth; there were three wrinkles. So I pull the sheets up, then pull them down—still, three wrinkles. Again, I pull the sheets up and then down. Four wrinkles. Whatever I do, the wrinkles keep showing up. The more I try, the more upset I become. Trying, trying, trying again. I feel like such a failure. Why can't I get it right?"

"Nicole, a wrinkle-free bed is strictly *your* version of perfection. Everybody's standard is different. What did you feel in your body when you were reproaching yourself?"

I let this set in for a few minutes.

"My stomach tightened, my breathing was stuck in my chest, and I heard my parents saying, 'Nicole, is this the best you can do?'" She stops to catch her breath. She rephrases what I just said. "So if perfection is in the eye of the beholder, I *am* the beholder. In that case, perfection is not an arbitrary definition dictated by my parents." From the light in her eyes, I can tell the information is getting through. "Is it really that simple?"

"Yes! Nicole, *you* are in charge of your thoughts, ideas, opinions, and most importantly, your actions."

"I can decide that ten wrinkles are fine?" she says with a teasing twinkle in her eyes.

"However many wrinkles are comfortable to you or not!"

"I need time to adjust to this after a lifetime of trusting the dictates of others."

Waving my arm in the air, I affirm, "Yes, you control *you*. It's enough for one day. Next time, we'll start your meditation practice."

For our first meditation session, we settle in a secluded spot under a big oak tree on the college campus. I explain that the word *meditation* comes from the Latin *meditare,* meaning "to think over, reflect, consider" and that the root *med* has something to do with actions that bring about healing.

Nicole listens intently. "Okay, I understand. Perhaps if I reflect *why* my inner voice is negative and overly critical, I can thwart the notions that I can't do anything correctly."

Delighted, I propose, "Let's see what happens when putting this theory into practice."

I introduce basic meditation techniques: how to sit and how to focus on the breath. Nicole is a quick learner. With her eyes closed and her shoulders and face relaxed, she looks like she is absorbed in a pleasant dream. When the soft sound of the chime announces her first eight-minute meditation is over, Nicole looks surprised.

"Thoughts continued to come as soon as I lost my connection to my breath, but as soon as I reconnected to my breath, I felt calm and untroubled. Quite amazing...I like feeling that way."

"Meditation pulls us out of our inner turmoil. It's like a brief respite. The divide between the successful and unsuccessful Nicole fades, and what emerges is the real Nicole who is competent, intelligent, and accomplished." I put into words what she just experienced during her meditation.

On our next meeting, Nicole can't wait to report, "These stress management techniques are really effective. Even my dog likes them." She laughs. "I'm up to fifteen minutes now. I still struggle with those deep yogic breaths before I meditate, but they do help dissolve my negative thinking. By the way, can I join your yoga class?"

"Absolutely! Yoga will release muscular tension and help your breathing, and you'll love deep relaxation. It's a wonderful decision for dealing with your stress level."

By the end of the summer, I broach the subject of bringing our impromptu sessions to an end. At an opportune moment,

I tell her how impressed I am with how much calmer and more content she is, and how much progress she has made in controlling her negative self-talk.

When parting after our last yoga class, Nicole hands me a yellow rose with coral overtones wrapped in soft white tissue paper with a red bow. "I appreciate what you've done for me. Things are not perfect," she says, smiling after the word *perfect,* a term we spent so much time dissecting, "but they're so much better than when we started. I never thought this would be possible, a transformed me. Meditation is my oasis of calm I look forward to each morning."

"It's been exciting to bring a bit of Yogaville to Plattsburgh," I say, smiling at the thought of how out of place the Lotus chapel would be on the Plattsburgh campus.

I arrange the rose in my Czech glass vase and place it in view of my yoga mat. A few days later when, I am about to throw out the dried-up rose, I notice tiny green shoots on the side of the stem. Amazed, I watch them grow from soft green shoots into bright-green baby leaves. Just like these bright shoots that have so unexpectedly burst into life, I have blossomed into a new *me* in my role as a yoga and meditation teacher.

In her thank-you card, Nicole wrote: "I remember walking into your home and almost gasping because of its calm beauty. I thought, here in this space created by this person, I can learn. And I did! It was a transformative experience." My mind returns to Yogaville's Lotus chapel, where I am basking in the energy of communal meditation. This time, Nicole is with us. Yogaville made the journey to Plattsburgh, where what I learned in the stress management training made a difference in one person's life, with more to follow in the years to come.

32: *My New Yoga Partner*

Rubbing one ear and looking a bit droopy, Dennis is watching me glide through a series of sun salutations from our bedroom doorway. His presence makes me self-conscious.

"Do you think yoga might help with this lingering cold?"

"Why don't you try it? I bet it would shake up the fluids in your head."

"And this nasty vertigo is driving me crazy."

"Even if it only distracts you from your misery, it's worth a try."

He mimics my sun salutation with less than perfect results. "I'm going to have to work at it," he says. "It's more difficult than I expected."

"For months, I couldn't get my back leg up to my hands in the lunge. Then one day, it just happened. No reason the same couldn't happen to you."

Dennis, true to his patient, conscientious character, tries out the sun salutation several times during the next few days. "Hey, I think I'm getting the hang of this. What else can I try?"

"How about triangle?"

He almost loses his balance but quickly floats back with an engaged look on his face. "Amazing, I felt the vertigo only on one side. I wonder what that means." A short time later, I catch him browsing through my collection of yoga books. "What do you recommend for learning about the benefits of the postures?" he asks.

Aha! I think. *He's hooked!*

Whether or not the yoga helped Dennis's cold and vertigo remains a question. What is certain, however, is that he did get better, with or without yoga, and his interest in yoga as both therapy and a physical challenge was aroused. Seizing the moment, I suggest we try a full practice. Hesitant but not really resisting, he says, "Okay, but only for half an hour." After a few warm-ups, I introduce warrior II, certain its strength-building qualities will appeal to him. He lifts his arms arrow-straight and anchors his legs into the carpet. "Wow. What power. More interesting than lifting weights." I'm delighted to see his pleasure. In deep relaxation, we curl into each other's arms, impressed with what we did. "This is fun," he whispers with a luminous look in his eyes.

Days later, the potato I am peeling almost slips out of my hand when Dennis asks tentatively, "Do you think I could join your yoga class?"

"Are you kidding? What a great idea!" His approaching birthday gives me an excuse to buy him a thick green yoga mat, not the gift he expects, but his chuckle tells me he approves.

After a few classes, he sums up his impressions. "My breathing is deeper, my muscle strength has increased, and I hold the postures with more ease. I'm really pleased."

"Yes," I say, "over time, the body adjusts. It only gets better. I feel as agile as I was in my twenties. Imagine how advanced we would be if we had started yoga then!" I give into a momentary wistfulness at the impossibility of turning time back.

One night, Dennis arrives home from work at 5:30 p.m. and goes upstairs to change into loose-fitting workout clothes. I light a candle, place the green and turquoise yoga mats side by side, and put on our favorite CD, *Yoga for Rebalancing Body, Mind & Spirit* with Todd Norian. I giggle when I feel the air currents from his strong arm and leg movements brush my skin. The serene, otherworldly expression on his face glows in our soft candlelight. He looks like a contemplative icon. We exchange smiles when I stretch my arms to touch his fingertips. Without resorting to words, we feel the strength of our bond.

On our backs in corpse pose, we hold hands while Todd Norian's voice transports us into a peaceful state. The dialogue in my head disperses once I surrender to the bliss of pure release. Todd Norian's vocal "ohm" brings the practice to a close. Instinctually, we fold in a tight hug that transcends the separateness necessitated by our daily routine. With arms around each other's waist, we move toward the kitchen. "So how was your day? Do you have class preparations?" he asks. Our voices are low, our body movements light and unrushed.

Midafternoon on a dreary fall day, I am grading papers and sipping chamomile tea to Yo-Yo Ma playing Bach's Cello Suite no. 1. The phone rings. It's Dennis. With no introductory remarks, he blurts, "Ann, what do you think about my applying for the Kripalu Teacher Training? I've been mulling this over for a while and feel the timing is perfect. We retire in December, and they have a February training session."

I steady myself against the edge of my desk before asking, "Seriously?"

"I'm not one hundred percent sure, but this is the right moment to act on that impulse. What do you think?"

"I'm in shock! Ecstatic! What a transition into retirement. Even better, we'll be on the same voyage!"

"That's the boost I need. Let's talk it through tonight." He leaves me standing there with the phone gripped tightly in my hand.

I twirl around the dining room table and then, to steady my whirling mind, I move to the window to watch the rusty-colored leaves float down the stream. Dennis's words cycle through me. My heart about to explode, I sprint into the kitchen to leaf through my cookbooks to find a recipe to turn the chicken tenders I was planning for dinner into a celebratory meal. While I chop, sauté, and simmer, I try to imagine Dennis at Kripalu. *Will he like it as much as I did? Is teaching yoga his thing? What a thrill to share my yoga experiences with him on a deeper level.*

"We approach yoga differently," I comment, toasting his decision later that evening. "You're interested in the postures and their physical benefits, which I am as well, but I'm also interested in how the postures affect my mental state and above all, how they are changing my relationship to myself."

"Hey, I don't discount how yoga affects you in other ways. I'm ready to explore and learn." Taking my hand, he looks into my eyes as he turns the conversation in a new direction. "In a few months, we'll be moving to Maine and a new home. How do you feel about being separated for a month in a town where we don't know a soul?"

By way of reply, I check the Kripalu catalog to see if there's something I can plug into while he's there. What I find is an opportunity in a selfless service program as a *seva*, which would allow me free room and board in exchange for assigned work. With a voice gaining in momentum, I read the description aloud to Dennis: "Work-exchange program designed for energetic individuals with a desire to contribute to daily operations of Kripalu. Join a community of spirited, fun volunteers exploring what it means to be fully alive through service as a spiritual practice. Contribute. Gain skills. Reflect. Grow." I look at Dennis. "It's right here!" I exclaim, waving the catalog in my hand. "I like the idea of giving something back to Kripalu for what Kripalu has given me. And we'll at least be in the same building!"

Everything was coming together: retirement, our move to Brunswick, Dennis's decision to become a yoga teacher, and my decision to go to Kripalu as a seva.

Weeks later, excited about this novel adventure, we step out of our Brunswick home to kick off our retirement and travel the 250 miles to the Kripalu Yoga Center. We arrive on February 27, 2005, on a clear day between two major snowstorms. Filled with admiration and love for what Dennis is undertaking, I skip down the hall to the seva woman's dorm on the ground floor after dropping him off at his room. I take one of the ten bunk beds by the window so I can watch the fuzzy white-tailed rabbits chasing each other in the bushes under my window. My assignment with a crew of fun-loving youngsters is in veggie prep. Eight hours a day we clean, sort, and chop organic vegetables and drain water out of big blocks of tofu for the chefs, who prepare healthy meals for hundreds of Kripalu guests every day. My white hair is an advantage—the youngsters never let me carry heavy bins, and they involve me in their deliberations about how to design their future.

They have fun initiating me, a lover of classical music, into their new-age music scene and introducing me to favorite singers I have never heard of. While we're busy shredding and chopping, the conversational bounce keeps our hands moving in rhythm with our engaged voices. I learn about their meditation practices; relationships with parents, friends, and lovers; career aspirations; hobbies; and personal interests. I feel a motherly love for these young people, who are building meaningful lives with such thoughtful earnestness.

Shy, sweet-looking Danny is a stark contrast to his outgoing girlfriend Beth. Both students at prestigious colleges, they chose to spend their spring break as sevas at Kripalu. Unlike his girlfriend, who has an established yoga practice, he finds that everything at Kripalu is new to him: practicing yoga, working in selfless service, and participating in the weekly circle where we are asked to talk about something that is important to us while others listen intently without commenting. When it is Danny's turn to speak, he focuses his eyes on the carpet and says in a shallow voice, "I'm having a great time. Thank you so much for this experience." His speech has no emotion, no revelations, definitely no tears or laughter. It is a very nice, proper thing to say, and no doubt true, but his heart is not in it.

When it is my turn, I say something insignificant and humorous to avoid getting into personal issues. When done, I look over at Danny to let him know that revealing my innermost thoughts is as trying for me as it is for him. Back in the kitchen, Danny needs to talk. "I am so mad at myself. I blew the opportunity to talk about something that's bothering me."

"There's always next week," I say.

When it is his turn next circle time, Danny lifts his head, his glowing eyes scanning the faces of his fellow sevas as if he is gearing up for a race.

"Last week, I was disappointed with myself. I've always been a 'good boy,' 'a good Jewish boy.'" We all smile but remain silent. "My parents expect me to become a lawyer. I'm in law school now, but I never asked myself if this is what *I* want."

His girlfriend gives him a loving look. I nod vigorously to acknowledge how impressed I am with his strong beginning. Around the circle, faces are supportive. A novice at this kind of probing, he is trying hard to say exactly what he feels. More words tumble out: "I need to know myself better. Something unfamiliar and scary is happening to me, but it feels right. I don't have the answers, but I'm leaving Kripalu questioning *how I want to live my life.* Thank you for being here to listen. Thank you for opening yourselves up so I could get myself to do it."

His shoulders hitch back as he fills his chest with a deep breath. He looks shy in a sweet, endearing way, completely vulnerable to the emotions welling up in him. The group, though silent, empathizes with his quest for personal truth. Fighting back my tears, I know how momentous this confession is for him to deliver and for me to witness. Danny had the courage to do what I could not do. Was I too proud? Frightened? Or unable to trust? Whatever the explanation, I know it is behavior that goes back to the earliest years of my life, and it is not going to change that quickly, if ever.

After the meeting, I go over to Danny. We hug. He whispers into my ear, "Thank you."

"Oh, no, Danny, this was all your own doing. I wish you well in your future. You'll be fine. You might even be a great lawyer someday."

We both laugh with tears in our eyes. He looks a bit taller when he walks toward the doorway. That evening, I watch Danny dance with his girlfriend to the Kripalu drummers. Creating his own steps, his arms are up in the air, his head tilted to the side, his legs bent and swaying. He looks like a beautiful bird in flight. Even at sixty-two, it is not too late to learn what Danny is learning in his twenties. My time to model Danny would not come that year, or the year after, but I continue to inch toward that liberating release in my own way and at my own pace.

I tap Dennis on his shoulder when I notice him hunched over a stack of index cards by a picture window in the main lobby.

His lips still moving, as if addressing imaginary students for his upcoming practice teach, he looks at me bleary-eyed and bewildered.

"Why don't you practice on me?" I suggest. "The Forest Room is empty. Let's give it a try." Remembering fondly all the incredible yoga classes I have had in this room, I show him my favorite spot near the window. "I always focus on those evergreens during my practice," I say as I point to the cluster of tall trees weighted down with dark green branches and dangling pine cones. I roll out my mat and get into easy pose, looking away so I do not make him self-conscious.

"I…" He stops and peruses his note cards and lesson plan. I smile. Clearing his throat, he says, "Come on your hands and knees in preparation for cat and dog." His tentativeness echoes through the empty room. Reaching for his note cards, he asks, "What comes next?"

"Look for the answer in your body and follow my movements to know if your cues are working."

"Okay," he murmurs, putting his note cards away. "Come on your spine with your knees bent and arms out like wings. Bring your knees toward the floor on the right." His voice gains momentum. As he begins to ad-lib, his voice grows more and more vibrant.

"That was great! You know the stuff cold. Good details about the physiology of the postures. One very small bit of advice—smile occasionally so your students don't realize you're a scared novice." Then I add, "Without a doubt, you're going to ace the exam. You already have the authority of a teacher."

Holding hands as we leave the Forest Room, I recall a recent evening at our ballroom dancing class after a draining day
of teaching three writing classes and Chekhov short stories in
a fiction class. "I'll never fit into my dancing shoes after standing in class so many hours. Oh, and that stack of papers on my
desk..." I whine as we leave the house. The stiff smile on Dennis's face annoys me.

In the car, he says, "It's no fun if you don't feel like going."
He sounds disappointed.

"Let's be quiet if we're going to be so edgy," I say, staring
out the window.

Twenty minutes later, my husband is twirling me to the instructor's commands as she sways her hips to a jazzy foxtrot:
"Long, short, short, long, pivot." My movements are tense, con-
stricted. My body resists the pressure of Dennis's forceful grip.
My legs feel lifeless, heavy. I sense from the impatient way he
holds me that he wants me to be more receptive to his movements, but my body is unyielding.

The instructor switches from a foxtrot to a sensual tango.
I submit to the gentle pressure of Dennis's hand on my lower
spine, which signals how I am to maneuver my body. Following his lead, we slip into a harmonious duet. After a breathtaking spin, my mood lightens. "I'm sorry I've been in a bad mood.
It's been a beast of a day."

The grip in his arm lets up a bit. A soft smile spreads across
his face. This time, it is genuine. I laugh. Carried across the
floor on the strength of our resuscitated bond, our eyes connect. We stop counting the steps. The tension in my shoulders

relaxes. My face softens. "I'm really glad to be here with you," I whisper in his ear. He pulls me closer.

The drive home is silent. My hand is tucked under his warm thigh; his eyes are focused on the road. We tango into the house and before falling asleep in each other's arms, I set the alarm for 5:00 a.m. so I can grade the papers waiting on my desk, the vibrations of tango music still echoing through me.

The memory of the two of us gliding across the dance floor fades. But the feeling of warmth and closeness from our yoga session does not. Dance dissolves those momentary emotions that distance me from what I truly feel the way fog lifts to unveil what has been hidden. "I just realized that sharing yoga brings us together the way dancing does," I say as we part outside the Forest Room. There is no need for further explanation. The squeeze of his hand and love in his eyes make my heart quiver.

Dennis has become my yoga equal in knowledge, skill, and enthusiasm as he is on the dance floor and in our academic pursuits. Since the days we met in the Cornell Slavic Studies program, where we shared a love of Russian literature and our diverse but also complementary Slavic backgrounds, we have been soul mates. Now, in our early sixties, we nurture a yoga partnership in the spacious yoga room on the second floor of our Brunswick home where we practice, design classes, meditate, and try out new routines. It is here, where through the language of yoga, like in the language of dance, I differentiate the real from the unreal, especially when the *real* is momentarily fogged over but still there.

Part V:

From Chaos to Clarity

Verily, verily, I say unto you, Except a corn of
Wheat fall into the ground and die, it abideth
Alone, but if it die, it bringeth forth much fruit.

John 12:24

33: But Israel?

"Are you in pain?" I ask my mother, who is hunched over in the corner of my couch, face strained, mouth tightly clasped, hands restlessly smoothing out the lines on her forehead.

"The chemo is making me queasy. It will pass." She pulls herself up and, trying to smile, says casually, "Ann, my time is limited. The ovarian cancer is progressing. What do you think about taking a trip to Israel with me?"

My breath stops as if I've been punched in the belly. I feel a clamp tightening around my heart.

"Abe and I met and married in Tel Aviv. We were so young, so in love," Belle goes on, her mouth now trending up, her eyes brighter.

"But Israel?" I manage to squeeze out of my compressed lungs.

I move to the window so Belle cannot see how upset I am. Faint images of Tel Aviv from black-and-white frayed photographs are displaced by vivid memories of Prague's medieval rooftops and Nad Rokoskou street, where I knew every shortcut and secret pathway.

"*Israel?*" I repeat, dragging the letters out until they sound like a distant bird call. "What matters to me is Prague. That's where I left my heart."

Belle's lips tighten. "Yes, Israel is my past. No chance you might consider this offer?"

"Prague calls to my soul, but Israel is no more than a dot on the map."

Wrapped in pain, Belle remains silent.

To soften the blow of my rejection, I elaborate. "Before falling asleep, I dream about being in Prague—running to catch a tram, **walking in rhythm of ringing church bells**, singing folk songs with my friends in Moravian wine cellars…" Choked up, I leave the rest unsaid.

Certain about the rightness of my decision, I once more shake my head with a vigorous *no*. Belle stares at the painting of a Czech village hanging on the wall of our Plattsburgh home. Reminiscent of Chagall, it was a gift from an artist friend of Abe's, a memory of what we were about to leave behind. It has an inscription: To Anička, Josef Jíra, 1963. When she turns away from the painting, **Belle puts her frail hand over mine.**

"I know how important Prague is to you. But I have no desire to go back." I wait for the shiver running through her body to subside. "Anyway, Czechoslovakia is now off-limits for political reasons," Belle says with a deep sigh.

"It won't be like that forever. I need to revisit Prague to confirm my past is not some fabrication of my imagination."

Her eyes brim with love; her voice pleads for understanding.

"We can't get around the deep divide between your past and mine. I stand firm—*no* Israel."

"Well, what matters is we have each other," Belle says in a resigned voice.

"Yes, and that our love survived that past," I say in a conciliatory voice.

She wraps her arms around my waist and presses her head against my chest. I stroke her soft, wrinkled cheek. We wait for the love we have for each other to eclipse our pain before we resume a conversation about the outing to a nearby park.

A few months later, Belle can barely walk from her bed to the bathroom. Thoughts of travel to Tel Aviv or Prague have been reduced to trips to the doctor and the hospital. Belle's end-of-life wish to return to the place where she met and married my father was never fulfilled, a regret I live with to this day. It was rare for Belle, a master at keeping her past and the sadness surrounding it to herself. Dennis and I made our first trip to Israel thirty-three years after her death. I had to imagine what it would have been like if Belle and I experienced it together. The trip was a bittersweet compensation for a decision that was too late to reverse.

34: *Prague Once Again*

The root of the word *Praha,* the Czech word for Prague, is *práh,* or "threshold." For me, it refers to a threshold between the Prague that lives on in my memory and the Prague I return to when I step off the airplane at Ruzyně airport with my husband and sons, ages fourteen and eleven. Twenty-one years have passed since I left this city. Back on these familiar streets, my head is spinning and my body is in a state of heightened alert. I am barely able to get enough oxygen into my lungs. My mouth is dry, and my eyes dart from one building to the next to verify if each matches the one stored in my memory.

Everything evokes a response: the sound of my shoes rubbing against the square cobblestones, the tram's bell, walking past my college building, the aroma of sizzling sausages and yeasty beer, and the scent of freshly baked rolls I used to munch on during my walk from school. The four of us weave in and out of the narrow Malá Strana streets with their low houses, orange tile rooftops, and frescoes of suns, violins, peacocks, and sheep above the doorways.

I grab hold of the closest lamppost to steady myself when I see a group of people throwing handfuls of rice on a jubilant young bride and groom, calling out, "Many years, good luck, much happiness!" It was a sunny day, like today, when Laura and Pavel got married at the New Town Hall on Staroměstké Náměstí only a few blocks away. When they appeared in the entrance of the Town Hall as husband and wife, they were showered with rice. The images of Laura's wedding grow stronger, along with the voices of my parents, Pavel's family, and their entourage of friends. Everywhere I turn, Prague brings up memories of the life I left behind: here is the café where my university friends and I spent hours debating, philosophizing, and sharing our joys and heartbreaks; here is the theater where I heard Ives Montand sing; here is the National Theatre where the arias of Dvořák and Smetana's operas ignited my lifelong love of opera; and here is the bookstore where I spent my translation earnings.

Laura's cautionary words about going back to Prague echo through my head. "Why put yourself through all that emotional turmoil? Accept that it's not part of our lives anymore." I remember how I defended my decision to return when I said, "I need to touch, see, and feel the presence of this city for it to become real again instead of relegating it to a ghostlike existence in my imagination." And now that I am back, I am finding it emotionally much more complicated than I had expected.

"Why don't we go back to the hotel? It's all too much, too fast. You're as pale as a sheet. Here, lean on me," Dennis says in a take-charge tone. Back in our hotel, the Zlatá Husa (the Golden Goose), with a heavy head and blurry eyes, I sink into the soft bed with a fluffy feather quilt and a square-shaped pillow that takes up half the bed. Dennis pulls the curtains to block out the sights and sounds of the city, and our sons quietly retreat to their next-door room. Rocking me in his arms as if I am sick, Dennis waits for me to calm down. When too drained to cry, I drift into a restless sleep.

The next day, I show them the hill where I broke my neighbor's wooden sled; the playground where I learned to ride a bike; the dairy store where they poured milk into my milk can with a big ladle; the bakery where I bought long loaves of rye bread I nibbled on before I reached home; the top floor of the Rokoska villa where we lived; my elementary school down the hill; the Kobylisy library where I checked out my weekly supply of books; and finally, my gymnasium in the next neighborhood called Libeň.

We tour the castle, the medieval city, and all the major historic landmarks. We go to the famous Špejbl and Hurvínek puppet theater, concert halls and restaurants, museums with national treasures and native artwork. I tell them about the history of the Gothic and Baroque churches sprinkled throughout the city, and I introduce them to traditional dumplings with pork and sauerkraut and pastries drowning in whipped cream.

By the end of our stay, I confide to Dennis, "Being here feels like I'm on a roller coaster that has gone out of control. When not in Prague, I long to be there; when here, I'm a passive observer but not part of current life the way I used to be. It's both painful and confusing." I leave the city surprised how quickly my happiness at returning birthed an unsettling confrontation between my former and present-day lives. Over the next decade, we make several trips back, each as intensely emotional and perplexing as the first one.

On one of those visits, when strolling along the Vltava River with the castle and Saint Vitus Cathedral in view, I make a pronouncement. "Dennis, I'm at a loss how to handle my feelings. When here, I feel split in two. I can't manage the turmoil it puts me through. It's time to close this part of my life. This should be our last trip here."

Dennis, who has come to love the city and the Czech language, quickly brings me back to reality. "You can't just wish your past away. Like it or not, this place is part of your history."

I stand on the embankment of the river for a long time, committing every detail of the castle to memory, as if I am a painter who will need to retrieve the image for future use. I ask Dennis in a tired, dispirited voice, "Is there a way of reconciling my past with my life in America? If so, I haven't found it."

Later that evening, we meet our friends Alena and Pavel in one of our favorite downtown restaurants. Despondent, I announce, "It saddens me, but this will be our last visit to Prague. Being here tears me apart. It's more than I can handle."

Pavel fumbles with his cigarette lighter but remains silent. Alena puts her arm on my shoulder, as if to protect me from further hurt. "Aničko, for years we've watched you struggle with your relationship to Prague. Whatever you decide, you'll always be part of this place," she says with an understanding look. "However, I have something that might change your mind." She reaches for her big black purse, and after rummaging in it, she jiggles a set of keys. "We own a tiny apartment in

Břevnov we bought as an investment. We're too busy to use it. You and Dennis can stay there anytime you want. We'll show you what a beautiful residential neighborhood it's in."

"Břevnov?" I pull the word out into a high-pitched question. "Where on earth is that?"

"It's an old neighborhood a short distance from the castle. We can drive over after dinner," Alena says resolutely.

Pavel parks by a six-story building with a wraparound balcony on the top floor. "Look up, Aničko. That's your balcony. You have a view of the Svatý Vít steeples and the Prague Castle. Could it be any more spectacular?" he says, proud to have figured out a way to get me back to Prague.

"Incredible! I'm speechless! Give me time. Whatever I decide, I'm deeply, deeply touched." I give them both a tight hug.

A few years later, Dennis and I are exploring the streets of Břevnov on a beautiful summer day. We pop into a local pastry shop where the cakes are made by the owner, each a piece of art. Over cappuccinos and open-faced sandwiches, called *chlebíčky*, I outline the difference between Břevnov and Kobylisy. "In Břevnov, I'm living in the present; in Kobylisy, I'm back in the past." I stir my coffee before I continue. "When I get off at the Kobylisy tram stop, I'm once again the little girl who lived there in the 1950s. I see that neighborhood not the way it is today, but the way it was when I lived there."

"What's it like to walk by the villa you lived in?" Dennis asks.

"I see the beady eyes of Zapletalová, the landlady, piercing through me as if she had the power to make me vanish. At least today, I understand she hated us because the Communists dispossessed them of their family home. At the time, I thought she was a mean old witch who hated children, particularly my sister and me."

"What about some of your good memories?"

"That would be sledding down the hill with my friends… playing games with the kids on my street…spending time in the Kobylisy library…"

"That's the stuff I remember when I go back to Yonkers. I still have ties to the place, but I guess you were completely cut off from it as if it never existed."

"Well, in Břevnov, I'm creating memories rooted in the present," I say, putting my hand in his. "The other day, the lady in the bakery asked me what year I left the country. To keep things simple, I told her I left in my youth. She gave me a warm, friendly smile, and then she complimented me on coming back to my homeland. What better welcome than to be treated as one of them?"

35: *Who Am I?*

Fifty years have passed since I was in the Světozor movie theater on Vodičková Street off Václavské náměstí. The marble staircase leading to the vestibule with Greek columns and a turquoise ceiling with gold trim have not changed. Even the little corner café is in the same spot.

What has changed are the non-propagandistic posters and modern art that reflects the artistic freedom we never had during the Communist days. The Soviet, Czech, and Eastern Bloc films my friends and I watched from our favorite row number ten seem like a distant unreality compared to the uncensored films being shown today. Presently, my husband and I are seated in row ten for the acclaimed German film *The White Band*.

Halfway through the film, the picture goes out of focus. Nobody tries to change the situation; neither do I. The jerky images and subtitles give me a headache. When the film is over, the audience sheepishly piles out of the movie theater except for two women and a man about my age.

Visibly aggravated, the man approaches the young usher. "Please tell the projectionist I want to talk to him."

Curious, I wait for the projectionist to show up. In a few minutes, a young man with uncombed hair dressed in a baggy T-shirt and shorts makes an appearance. Furious, the older man confronts him. "Where were you? Why weren't you doing your job? Didn't you know the film was out of focus?"

Indifferent, the projectionist replies, "I was in the other theater."

"Well, I, for one, will not be returning to this theater anytime soon."

Silent until now, I explode. *"I'm an American.* In America," I continue, clenching my teeth and raising my voice, "if one delivers poor service, the customer is compensated. The least you can do is give us our money back, and an apology would be appropriate."

The projectionist shrugs his shoulders and starts walking toward the exit. I charge out of the darkened theater, my heart beating to the rhythm of my wrath.

Back on the street, Dennis asks, "What got you so angry?"

"It had more to do with me than the projectionist."

"What do you mean?"

"When I lived here, I was trained to suppress my individual voice. This was incompatible with the American emphasis on asserting your individuality. Even today, twenty years since the fall of Communism, only one man out of the entire audience spoke up—that is, until I joined him. The rest of the audience shuffled out like sheep, the way I used to. Who knows, this man might have been a rebel in his day."

"You sure let your voice be heard when you belted out 'I'm an American!'"

It took that one short, startling sentence for me to recognize that I no longer act or think like the Czech I used to be—instead, I act and think like the *American* I am now.

"How about a glass of wine in that cozy wine bar on Haštalská Street to toast my American wife?"

Strange how in a darkened Prague movie house, I recognized a truth I resisted accepting most of my life.

36: Prague in Black and White

The Museum of Communism opened in 2001 on the promi-
nent Příkopy Street in downtown Prague on the upper floor
of a building above McDonald's. Over the next ten years,
whenever I pass by, I recoil at the thought of returning to the
period of Czech history that overlaps with mine. Then, on a
visit in 2011, avoidance turns to curiosity, and eventually to
a decision.

"I can't hold back any longer," I say to Dennis. "It's time to
see if it's the way *I* remember it."

"I've been waiting for this day to come," he says.

We follow the signs pointing toward a dark passageway
with a spiral stone staircase adorned with an intricate metal
railing. It leads to the entrance of what was a nobleman's palace before the Communist takeover in 1948. The first room
sets the tone for the period with familiar images and relics:
red stars, hammers and sickles, Soviet flags, and banners with
upbeat slogans: "We are living better, happier lives, With the
Soviet Union forever." There are the familiar portraits of Stalin
receiving flowers from smiling Pioneers and statues of Lenin
holding a book of his revolutionary writing in an outstretched

hand pointing toward a glorious future. In my day, every square, official building, school, factory, store, and stadium had banners affirming the strong bond with our big brother, the Soviet Union. Evidence of that ideological intoxication is in every photograph of 1950s Prague. What a fantasy world they created, I realize.

The only visitors in the museum, I feel we are in the chambers of a secret society that has gone underground. There are video displays of radiant workers speed-piling bricks to over-fulfill the projected five-year plan; smiling peasants working in the fields; Pioneers waving Czech and Soviet flags in the May Day parade; members of the Communist Youth organization harvesting sugar beets and picking hops; and newspaper clippings gloating over the Communist victory in eradicating bourgeois values. It all brings me back to the days when Party functionaries upheld the power of the collective.

The exhibits explain the rise of Communism, how it functioned, and why and how it collapsed. Motionless wax figures and black-and-white period photographs tell the unpublicized stories of food shortages, the Slánský show trials, the brutal enforcement of collectivization, the confiscation of private properties and businesses, the enforced nationalization of the industry, and the political indoctrination of the youth at rallies and brigades. Upbeat melodies of songs glorifying the col lective mute the sound of the creaking parquet floors under our feet as we shuffle from room to room. Personal accounts of people who risked their lives to illegally cross the border to the West clash with the "glorious socialist future" the Czech people were promised by Lenin, Stalin, and Gottwald (the first Czechoslovak Communist president).

We study pictures of the Spartakiáda, a mass sports event that showcased the unity of the Eastern Bloc countries, which I participated in when I was a Pioneer. I smile at the memory of what happened on that historic day. "After waiting in the blistering sun to enter the stadium, I fainted. I was treated for sunstroke and sent home in an ambulance. After months of rigorous practice, I never got to perform in these stylish outfits," I tell Dennis, pointing to a black-and-white photograph of schoolgirls in tight-fitting tops and short pleated skirts. "I was so disappointed!"

More memories trickle back at a photograph of Pioneers entering the mausoleum to pay their respects to the deceased president. They claimed he died of pneumonia he caught at Stalin's funeral. He actually suffered from syphilis and alcoholism and died of a burst artery. Oh, the lies they fed us!

"What you lived through is a cautionary lesson for future generations," Dennis says in a hollow voice.

"Manipulated truths, lies, distorted realities—that's what defines this horrific period."

My heart stops when we enter a room with a mannequin of a twelve-year-old girl in a dark skirt, white shirt, and red Pioneer scarf seated at a typical fifties desk with an inkwell and storage space under the desktop. She is looking adoringly at portraits of Stalin and Gottwald.

"That's what I was like," I say in a strained voice.

"Did you really idealize these leaders that much?"

Disheartened by the memory of my former self, I concede, "Sad, but yes. I had complete, unquestioning trust they only meant the best for us. Isn't that awful?"

"How can you reproach yourself for sponging up an ideology that was drilled into you at home, in school, on the radio, and in the newspapers? What choice did you have? You eventually discovered the truth the hard way."

The displays in the last two rooms are devoted to images of the Prague Spring when the Czechs and Slovaks tried to humanize the Communist system; photos of the 1968 Soviet invasion that squelched those efforts; the underground resistance movement; and the self-immolation of Jan Palach to protest the invasion. Wall-to-ceiling photographs of the 1989 Velvet Revolution when the Czechs took over Václavské Náměstí, shaking their keys to mark the start of a new, post-Communist era, bring the Communist experiment to a close.

"I've had enough. I need some fresh air," I say. "I wonder how Belle and Abe would feel about the role they played in this drama. And Laura, who never wants to remember any of this." I glance one last time at this vanished world.

The museum attendant, too young to have lived through the Communist era, asks cheerfully, "What did you think of the exhibits?"

"It shows how it was. It's not possible to revisit those days without getting emotional, especially if you lived through it."

The young woman nods as if she understands.

Interested, I ask, "Who visits the museum?"

"A trickle of foreign visitors curious about life under Communism, but mostly teachers bring schoolchildren to teach them about that past. Some parents, ashamed of things they did to get ahead or to survive, avoid talking about those years. There are still unhealed scars and wounds. To heal from a past like that, we must be sure not to forget!"

"There are both collective wounds and personal ones. It's a reality that will always be with us, whether we face it or not," I say before we make our way to the exit door where a transformed, and ever lovely Prague, awaits us.

During a May 2013 visit, Dennis and I stay in a fourth-floor apartment that belongs to Pavel's mother, who is in a nursing home. It is in a turn-of-the-century building in the Letná section of Prague. The scent of lilacs coming through the open window reminds me of my twentieth birthday on May 19, when Belle handed me a spectacular bouquet of the white and purple lilacs that were blooming throughout Prague. From that day on, I associated my birthday with the fragrance of those blooming lilac bushes, and with Prague.

Back in present-day Prague, I am on my purple travel mat stretching my arms toward the ceiling. My eyes shift from the purple and white lilac bouquet Dennis gave me for my seventy-first birthday to two cats, one black and one white, perched on the ledge of the apartment building across the street. The playful pitch-black cat intertwines itself with the snowy white one. The pair becomes grayscale, then morphs to monochrome. Separating again, the black and white bodies become distinct, then they merge anew, bodies rubbing against each other before retreating once more into their own spheres. They perform a sensual dance of opposites—now together, now separate, now somewhere in between.

What I see in the interplay of their moving seems an emblem of the inner tension between my Prague past and Brunswick present. The black cat, amorphous and hard to delineate, is like my past shrouded in mystery, in contrast to the white one, which reflects the greater simplicity and stability of my current life. The balls of blackness and whiteness blend, creating a glacial white ball with black-edged tinges and then a charcoal black ball with specks of white. As the two animals become one cat, one color, for less than a minute, the distinction disappears, then reappears. Reality is altered; even so, change continues. Nothing lasts, nothing is forever, like Shiva's dance that shuttles back and forth between the states of destruction and creation. Life's only certainty is change and interchange. In this dance, past and present coexist without obliterating each other. The image of the interplay of the black and white cats invades my subconscious.

The day before our departure, Dennis and I visit a memorial built in 2002 to commemorate victims of the Communist era. A plaque at the foot of the statue states it "is dedicated to all victims, not only those who were jailed or executed, but also those whose lives were ruined by totalitarian despotism." Perhaps not ruined, but affected, I am mortified to see that the bronze figures replicate portions of my experience.

The memorial consists of seven naked bronze figures on a flight of ascending stairs. Each figure is a statement showing how Communism diminished, broke, splintered, and ultimately devastated body and spirit. We first see a chest split in half, then lost limbs, and a body without a head, which documents the process of human devaluation and loss of selfhood. The last figure only has a pair of legs without a torso or head. The head, heart, and soul have been demolished, canceled. Each figure reminds us of the brutal violation of the human spirit that leaves nothing but a memory of what had once been there.

My legs feel like I am nailed to the ground. I cannot take my eyes off the gaping split in the chest of one of the figures that says so much more than words possibly could.

"After forty years of obliteration and diminishment, the Czechs are restoring and rebuilding as individuals, and as a nation," I say to Dennis in a shaky voice.

"It will take more than a generation to overcome this past," Dennis says as he waves in the direction of the memorial, "because the wounds still live in the told and untold stories of each family."

And in its own small way, the story of my family belongs to the told and untold stories from the rise and fall of the big Communist experiment that left the lives of millions shattered in its aftermath. *All* survivors have had to mend the upheaval it created both in their private lives and in their connection to society.

Back in my Brunswick home, I replay the image of the black and white cats blending into their fanciful embrace. The polarities of black and white, day and night, light and dark have this magical moment when they are neither distinctly one or the other. They hover in a twilight zone to create something that does not yet exist. Yogis call this process of transformation the life force or *prana*.

When *prana* is awakened, it paves the way to a new reality. Call it reconciliation, healing, or a merger of former selves, this is what these repeated trips to Prague have been for me: a weaving of what has been lost into what has been found. I liken this process to the creation of a quilt. When I sew small triangles and squares into blocks that I join together with borders and connecting sashes, I am in awe at how it comes together to form a cohesive quilt. It has been the same process with the formation of my present-day self, a weaving together of all I have lived through.

Prague has become, for Dennis and me, a home away from home. We thrive on walks through our favorite medieval streets and visits to restaurants, pubs, bookstores, theaters, movie houses, museums, wine cellars, cafés, and parks. We visit art galleries and frequent dance halls where brass bands crank out timeless songs my generation, and generations before us, danced and sang to. As I look at the older couples in a fast-twirling polka, I wonder which of the men, if I had stayed behind, might have become my husband. I sing along with the band as if I never left, surprised that the words and tunes are still intact in my memory's archive.

37: Full Circle

"Ann, did you see Kripalu's latest catalog? Shobhan and Sudhir's workshop, Energy Intensive, is going to explore the relationship between energy and consciousness. I can't resist it. Any chance you might join me?" Joy's voice sings out at the other end of the phone.

"I'll take anything with Shobhan," I tell her. "Besides, what fun to do this together!"

Returning to Kripalu after a prolonged absence, I expect everything to be the same. Instead, Buddha's statue in the main lobby and the dancing Shiva in the Shadowbrook Room are gone. The dorm rooms that never had locks are now opened with plastic coded cards. *Have there been some thefts?* I wonder. Coffee, the forbidden drink, is available outside the Kripalu shop, and the dining hall offers chicken and fish alongside its vegetarian dishes. The Kripalu shop has a new line of upscale yoga clothes and gift items, and in the practice rooms, mats previously squeezed into closets are neatly hung on hooks. Fortunately, these cosmetic changes have not changed the spirit of the place or the tangible and intangible experiences etched in my mind.

Joy and I arrive on the same day at the same time, she from Ohio and I from Maine. We pick up where we left off with natural ease. Returning to the Shadowbrook Room for an afternoon yoga practice triggers an overview of the changes in my life since I became a yoga teacher. "We lived through so much in this room. And so many good things have happened since I've walked out of here," I note as I arrange my yoga mat in front of the skeleton.

"It's been eleven years," Joy says, raising her eyebrows. "Look how we're expanding our horizons—integrative breath work, blocked energy, moving prana, a whole new yoga universe! Maybe it will reveal things we still don't know about ourselves." The twinkle in her eyes matches her same infectious smile.

In the opening lecture, Sudhir and Shobhan discuss the interrelationship between energy, awareness, and breath work. Moved by how much this relates to my own experience, I take furious notes: "When our inner flow of energy and awareness is blocked or out of balance, we experience separation from our true nature. As we release into the flow of energy and awareness, we return to a natural state of harmony and balance. Balancing and awareness is the Kripalu path." I scribble in the margin, "That is exactly how Kripalu has turned my life around."

The next day, Sudhir gets us settled for the crowning one-hour exercise of circular breathing. I have heard so much about it, from "It will blow your mind" to "It's like a trip to another planet." I am nervous. I am excited. But above all, I am curious what this will do to me. Lying on my spine, I pull the blanket up to my chin, and lowering my arms alongside my body, I press my shoulder blades and hips into the blue blanket underneath me. *What will happen?* Sudhir's voice, rising above the soft music, instructs us to connect our in-breaths with our out-breaths in a circular pattern without a pause in between. A continuous chain of breaths is moving through me in a train-like rhythm: *chug-a-lug, chug-a-lug, chug-a-lug.*

It doesn't take long before piercing cries and shouts echo through the room in response to our circular breathing. Fully focused on not interrupting the cycle of circular breaths, I have no energy to react to those sounds. My brain commands: *Breathe in. Breathe out. Breathe in. Breathe out.* I am aware of one thing only: the strong pulses of my rising and falling chest and the continuous flow of uninterrupted deep breaths. I can't think. I can't fantasize. I can only feel the intensity of the moment as if I am spinning to the melody of an intoxicating polka.

When Keith, an assistant kneeling by my head, sees my stamina waning, he encourages me in a soft voice, "Ann, relax. Give in to this experience. Don't fight it. Let go."

As in a fog, I hear the words *experience* then *fight,* but my comprehension blurs before I can register their meaning. My lower lip trembles, tears roll down my cheeks, and deep-seated sadness envelopes me. How long has this grief been buried? Building to a crescendo, I never let up on pushing the circular breaths out of my thundering lungs. I am a floating helium balloon. Miraculously, the separation between my mind and my body has been erased.

Abruptly, a single word, *alone, alone, alone,* like a distant foghorn preventing ships from crashing into invisible rocks, reverberates through me. Melancholy floods my being. I tremble as tears come and go. My mouth is dry and my body is drained, as if I swam from one side of a wide river to another without a moment's rest.

Sudhir brings this experience to a close. My mind a blank, tears of relief are unstoppable as a heavy grief lifts and then dissolves. Shobhan's voice reaches me from far away. "Ann, are you all right? Do you want to talk?"

Submerged in a vast expanse of unexplored space, my shoulders soften, burrowing into the blanket. I shake my head *no.*

Something I can't name or understand split open in me. I wait. Slowly, I lift my heavy eyelids. The bodies moving around me look like shadows that are out of focus. The overhead lights hurt my eyes. Muted sounds reach me in waves, as if my head is underwater. Shobhan advises, "Don't be in a rush to return to activity. Give yourself time to integrate your experience."

I inch toward the door, unsteady and vulnerable. Keith cautions, "Ann, take it slowly." I continue to move toward the door at a snail's pace. Clinging to the wall, I maneuver down the crowded hall like a sailor on a rocking ship.

Back in the dorm, shell-shocked and glassy-eyed, Joy is putting on her jacket and hat. "Let's have a silent walk. Fresh air will bring us back to the here and now."

"Okay. Yes to walking, no to talking." When we reach the stone gate by the Kripalu entrance, I inquire, "Ready to talk?"

"A painful past event came to me with a different ending. It changed my understanding of that event. It was nothing short of a miracle."

"You look relieved, radiant."

"You also look like something important happened."

"*Najdeš* is my explanation."

"Oh, yes! I remember this word came to you during deep relaxation in Michael's practice teach during our training."

Nodding, I add, "In Czech, it means 'you will find.' It must have a connection to the word *alone* that appeared during today's circular breathing in English."

"What could it be?"

I'm beginning to connect the puzzle pieces. "The word *alone* is the missing piece."

"How so?"

"True, I was *alone* in dealing with my conflicts, but it also made a fighter out of me. And with yoga as my beacon, I mended what was separated in me, thus one word in Czech and the other in English." Bursting into dance, I sing to a made-up melody, "I've come full circle." And then a bit louder: "I've come full circle! *I've come full circle!*"

Joy hums along, waving her hand in the air. "Is this what circular breathing did to you? I'll have to get a leash to rein you in."

"This is what finding my way out of a haunted forest does to me." My dance completed, I say seriously, "An hour of circular breathing dislodged the last remnants of buried grief. It felt like an electric shock entered through my feet and came out through the crown of my head, leaving me grief-free."

When asked to write a letter to the child within me on the last day of the workshop, I give the advice I wish I had received as a child: "Don't let others make you feel that your feelings are unimportant—take ownership of them. Otherwise, you'll have to work through the pain to bring up those buried feelings.... When you feel yourself pushing the wave of feeling away, stay with it. When you allow yourself to feel what you are suppressing, you are on the path of transformation."

The reminder that change begins with a single seed, illustrated by the chickpea that Yoganand gave us at our graduation ceremony, has proven true. Step by step, moment by moment, stretch by stretch, breath by breath, month after month, year after year, I have been healing from the divisions that have prevented me from feeling whole. In this Energy Intensive workshop, that seed matured into a firmly rooted tree.

Epilogue

PROCLAIMING PRESENCES
I am. I was here.
I leave marks, signs, meanings.
A meaning. I signify. I imply. I fly.
Decipher the foot-writing of a reading of the sky.
the sea, the air, the sand, the land...

Unfinished poem by Abe Chapman
Stevens Point Wisconsin, Intensive Care Unit, 1976

May 19, 2021
Dear Abe and Belle:
Today is my birthday. Can you believe your baby daughter is seventy-nine years old? Soon it will be fifty years since I shared my life with you in frequent conversations and visits. So much has happened. So much has changed. So much continues to live on in my memory.

This memoir is my way of updating you on my current life. Through writing, I have gained a better understanding of why yoga swept me off my feet and how it is related to our joint past. I discovered I have been two Anns: the little girl whose life started in America and the other one whisked away to a secret life in exile. The result *split me,* tore me between two languages, cultures, and belief systems. Though belatedly, I can only guess how painful it was for you to watch my American identity atrophy during our years of exile. This makes it particularly sad that you did not live to see how yoga helped me reconcile that split.

Despite setbacks and detours, I emerged from the messiness of our past stronger and more self-sufficient. The love of life, art, literature, and music that you transmitted to me has been a treasured gift. I have relied on that rich inheritance and grown through it. One thing I never doubted—your love for Laura and me was steadfast, which does not mean we lived without conflict, sorrow, and regret. It is the love we had for each other that enabled us to get through the hard times.

Abe, these lines you wrote with a weakening heart have become my motto for a purposeful life:

I am. I was here....I signify. I imply. I fly.

Until your last breath, you never stopped questioning, probing, and wondering. The expansiveness of your reach and your awe in deciphering life's mystery come across when you write:

Decipher the foot-writing of a reading of the sky,
the sea, the air, the sand, the land...

It is this passion for words, poetry, and music—your drive to express thoughts and feelings in writing—that inspired me to put pen to paper in search of my own story. Most importantly, you taught me there is a world larger than my own waiting to be discovered.

From you, Belle, I learned to face adversities; you also modeled the importance of bringing people together over a good meal and masterful conversation. Remember the day it poured when we planned a picnic with friends? Without a moment's hesitation, you spread a large tablecloth on the living room floor, thus showing me there's always an alternative. When I was in despair over how to make up two lost years of my Czech education, your faith in me helped me through. Your practical actions and joyful spirit got our family through many calamities. Time and again, you showed me how to keep going when the future seemed hopeless.

Abe and Belle, in your youth, your energies were outwardly directed toward radical social action. I turned my energies inward so I could make changes on a personal level. Your fighting spirit was aimed at redesigning the world. My personal revolution was aimed at making peace with my restless soul. That is what to "signify, imply, and fly" has meant to me.

Together, you set my life into a wild spin, which made it hard to discern where your story ended and mine began. Yoga showed me a way out of that confusion. You would be pleased to know I have transformed my past from an impediment to an asset. Our story of struggles, transformations, and reconciliations lives on in this memoir—for us and the future generations.

With much love, your daughter,

Ann, then Anička, then again Ann

Acknowledgments

This memoir has had a long journey. Along the way many people contributed their time, expertise, and advice. My thanks to Victoria Alexander, Joy Bush, Marlis Cambon, Claire Denenberg, Susan Mikesell, Diane Paterson, Helen Reagan, Eli Rosenberg, and Claudia Steinberg for reading earlier drafts of this manuscript and for suggesting ways to improve it. Special thanks to Eli Rosenberg for bringing Bessel Van Der Kolk's book, The Body Keeps the Score, to my attention at a crucial stage of my writing. Heartfelt thanks to Laurie Baden, Kathleen Canrinus, Elizabeth Fitting, Mary Jane Gonzalez, Ortolano Leonard, Kathryn Maller, Ken Rhee, and Linda Seeman from Molly Tinsley's Creative Writing Class for their honest, and constructive feedback. They made sure I never forgot to write with the reader's perspective in mind.

Karetta Hubbard's unshakable faith in the worth of my story and her supportive presence sustained me through numerous drafts. Karetta's edits significantly strengthened how I described the connection between my life before and after yoga. Thank you for your imaginative guidance.

Molly Tinsley's creative writing class and her superb edits

encouraged me to trust my intuition and delve deeper into how yoga transformed my attitudes and responses to life's challenges. Each batch of edits showed me that less is more and that finding just the right word in the right place can turn the ordinary into the extraordinary.

Holly Moir's meticulous edits and keen eye for detail brought a final shine to the manuscript.

Ray Rhamey's willingness to explore multiple possibilities until the cover captured the essence of my story, and his creative approach to honoring the spirit of the manuscript made our collaboration a gratifying experience.

I am deeply indebted to my yoga teachers, whose soulful teaching and contagious passion for yoga opened me to a deeper understanding of myself. I am grateful to my yoga students for allowing me to share my love of yoga and my faith that yoga I thrived on the encouragement and support of my husband Dennis. Our discussions about my childhood and early years after my return to the States were pivotal in shaping the chaos of what I had lived into a coherent story. I am grateful for the time he gave me to write, for his imaginative meals and intellectual input that nourished both my creativity and our relationship.

About the Author

Ann Kimmage, author of *Split in Two: Reconciled Through Yoga*, is a former adjunct faculty member in the English Department at Plattsburgh State University. Her memoir, *An Un-American Childhood*, was published in 1996 by University of Georgia Press, and her essay, "Growing Up in Exile" was published by University of Illinois Press in 1998 in the anthology *Red Diapers: Growing Up in the Communist Left*, edited by Judy Kaplan and Linn Shapiro. She retired to Brunswick, Maine with her husband where she has taught yoga classes at a variety of venues, Pilates, Meditation, literature classes at the local Senior College, Memoir Writing classes, learned how to quilt, and returned to memoir writing.